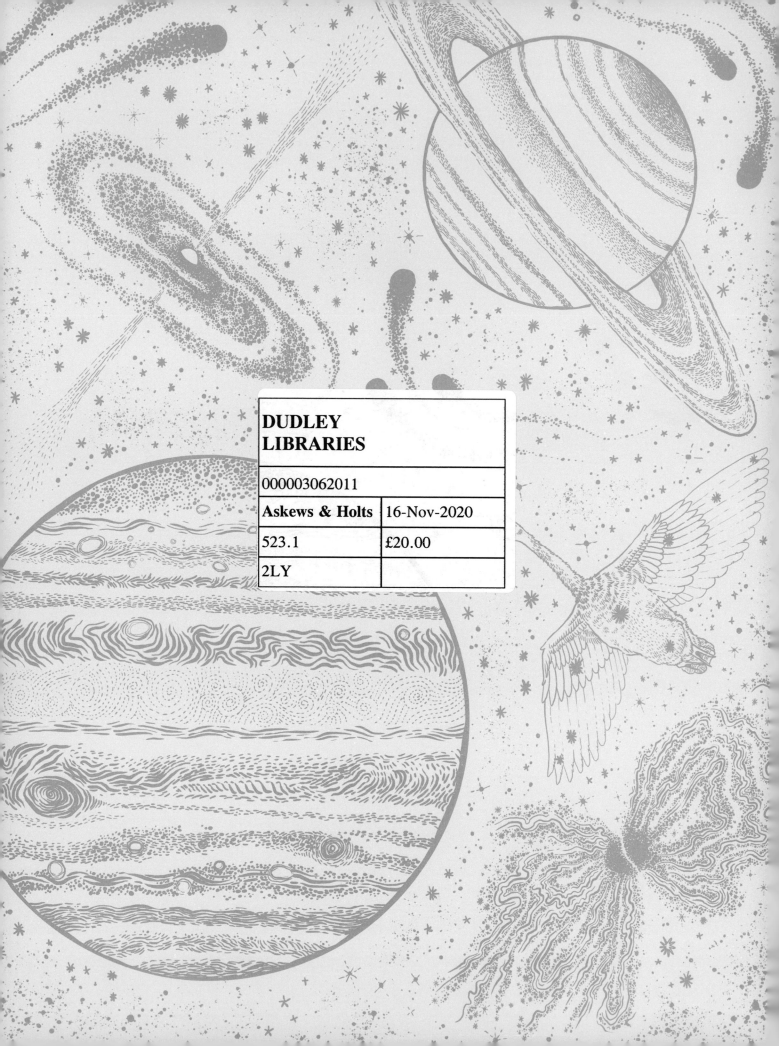

THE MYSTERIES
OF THE
Universe

Written by Will Gater

Illustrated by Angela Rizza
and Daniel Long

Introduction

Are you ready to go on an adventure? As you turn the pages of this book you'll be following in the footsteps of countless adventurers, scientists, and stargazers who have wondered at the great mysteries of the Universe. The journey will begin on our home planet, Earth, a marvel all in itself, and continue further and further into space, to the planets of our Solar System and out to the stars and galaxies beyond. As you meet some of the most extraordinary objects in the cosmos, you'll learn all about what they are and how astronomers study them, and you'll also see that there's lots we still don't understand — many mysteries are yet to be solved!

Now, let's get going!

Will Gater

Will Gater
Author

Contents

Earth's atmosphere

Our atmosphere might only be a thin veil of gas that clings to our planet, but it allows us to live here, and it is where many beautiful celestial sights, such as meteors and auroras, are created.

When we look up on a clear day, the sky glows a vibrant shade of blue. This is because the gases in the air scatter the bluer colours in the sunlight. When night falls, we can see another effect of the atmosphere: the gentle twinkling of the stars. This flickering happens because the moving air above us briefly distorts the path starlight takes to reach our eyes.

Our atmosphere is mostly made up of nitrogen, with smaller amounts of other gases such as oxygen and carbon dioxide.

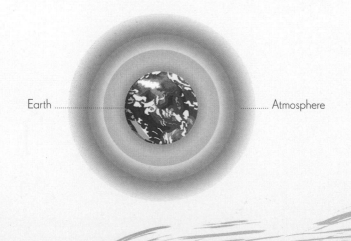

Earth .... Atmosphere

Noctilucent, or "night shining", clouds are only visible at twilight.

The night sky

Humans first turned telescopes toward the night sky around 400 years ago.

This dazzling view is from the Atacama Desert in Chile.

Every evening, as darkness falls and the sky turns from deep blue to inky black, the wider cosmos comes into view. Glittering stars fill the sky to form a sparkling backdrop for the planets that sail above our heads. Occasionally, a meteor zips across the scene, while night after night the Moon's silvery face slowly cycles through its phases.

Today, astronomers use powerful telescopes to peer deep into space, enabling us to explore the very distant Universe. Here, there are billions of galaxies, each full of countless stars. Perhaps in one of them there's someone else looking up, marvelling at the magic of their own twinkling night sky!

Meteors

Have you ever spotted a shooting star? These fleeting streaks of light are formed when a tiny piece of space dust — usually about the size of a grain of sand — hits our atmosphere. The flecks of dust themselves are strewn throughout the Solar System, and when they collide with Earth some are travelling at speeds as fast as 240,000 km (150,000 miles) per hour.

As the dust crashes into our atmosphere it squishes the air, causing the gas in front of it to heat up. In a split second, the dusty grain begins glowing and is quickly vaporized as it races across the sky — this is what we see as a shooting star, or to use its scientific name, a meteor.

Meteor showers - when meteors streak from the same point in the sky - occur when Earth passes through a trail of dust left behind by a comet or asteroid.

A bright meteor falling during the Geminid meteor shower, which occurs every December.

This meteorite was discovered in Chile's Atacama Desert.

Meteorites

Sometimes a space rock is so big that if it hits Earth's atmosphere it can survive its fiery journey through our skies without being totally destroyed. When a chunk of cosmic debris lands on the ground, it is called a meteorite.

Meteorites come in many different forms. Some are stony, while others are made mostly of metals, such as iron and nickel. Scientists regularly scour deserts and other remote areas, such as Antarctica, looking for meteorites. This is because studying them tells us about what distant Solar System objects are made of, and can reveal the hidden history of the planets.

Some meteorites are actually pieces of the Moon and Mars.

Auroras

On most evenings when darkness falls over the Earth's polar regions, softly glowing curtains of light called auroras appear against the black. Sometimes these displays ripple overhead, bursting across the sky with bright, colourful rays. In the northern hemisphere they are called the Northern Lights, or the aurora borealis, and in the southern hemisphere they are known as the Southern Lights – the aurora australis.

These dancing strips of mainly green and red are created when the Earth's magnetic field – energised by the wind flowing from our Sun – funnels charged particles into our atmosphere. We can't see them with our eyes, but as they rain down into a vast ring-shaped swathe of the atmosphere around the poles, they make the gases there glow.

Aurora borealis

Aurora australis

The green colour of auroras
comes from glowing
oxygen gas.

A view of the aurora
borealis, taken from
the International
Space Station

The constellation Orion is named after a hunter in Greek mythology.

Constellations

Have you ever spotted a familiar outline or shape in the sparkling stars of the night sky? You're not alone. For thousands of years, sky-watchers from cultures all over the world have picked out patterns in the stars, called constellations. Today, the International Astronomical Union recognizes 88 constellations. These represent all sorts of objects and creatures, as well as mythical figures — (see pp. 200–203). Star shapes that aren't official constellations, such as the Plough and the Summer Triangle, are called asterisms.

Most of the constellations that are visible in the night sky change with the seasons, as the Earth moves around the Sun. This means the stars we see in summer are different to those on show in winter.

This is the constellation Orion. Can you spot his belt?

The Moon

Gaze up at the Moon on a clear night and you'll be looking at an object that has billions of years of history etched into its surface. Its cratered landscape tells the story of countless asteroid and comet impacts long ago in the lifetime of the Solar System. But how did this ball of rock end up orbiting Earth? That's something that puzzles scientists even today. The most popular theory is that around 4.5 billion years ago, the young Earth collided with another world — the impact was so violent that this second world was destroyed, and huge amounts of hot, molten material were blasted into space. Eventually, the debris clumped together and cooled, and the Moon was born.

Earth

Moon

When the Moon is furthest from Earth, you could place the seven other planets in the space between!

This image shows the Moon crossing the sunlit side of our home planet.

Phases of the Moon

Waxing crescent

First quarter

Waxing gibbous

Full moon

Y ou have probably noticed that the Moon looks as if it is always changing shape. Sometimes it looks like a banana, while other times it's round, like a dinner plate. Sometimes it is somewhere between the two. These changing shapes are known as the phases of the Moon.

The phases happen because the Moon is constantly moving around the Earth. This means the amount of its face that's lit up by sunlight changes night after night. The Moon is spinning too, but we only ever see one side of it because it rotates on its axis in about the same amount of time as it takes to zoom around our planet!

The dividing line between the sunlit part
and the dark part of the Moon's face
is known as the terminator.

Waning gibbous

Third quarter

Waning crescent

New moon

The moon rotates on
its axis as it moves
around the Earth.

A total lunar eclipse can reveal stars that
are usually hidden by the Moon's glow.

Lunar eclipse

Did you know that sometimes the Moon turns a stunning shade of red? Well, it's not the Moon itself that changes colour, although it might look that way. It's all down to the Earth's atmosphere and our planet's shadow.

Very occasionally, the Earth, the Sun, and the Moon are aligned in such a way that Earth casts a shadow over a full Moon. When this happens, the Moon's silvery-white face gradually darkens, in what astronomers call a total lunar eclipse. Yet even in full shadow, the Moon doesn't disappear from view. That's where Earth's atmosphere comes in! Our skies filter the sunlight passing through them, leaving only redder colours to make it out into space. Not only that, but the atmosphere also bends that reddish glow into the gloom of our planet's shadow. The result: a copper-coloured full Moon hanging in the sky.

The full Moon turns a beautiful red during a total lunar eclipse.

The light of Earthshine takes about 1.3 seconds to travel from our planet to the Moon.

Earthshine

Everyone knows that the Earth doesn't shine... or does it? Take a look at a thin, crescent Moon. You'd expect the rest of its round face to be hidden in darkness, as it is night on that part of its surface and no sunlight is reaching there. But look carefully and you will see that the whole Moon is faintly lit up. Believe it or not, our planet is responsible!

When the Sun shines on the Earth's clouds and oceans, they send some of that light back out into space in different directions. This Earthshine can reach our neighbour, where it illuminates the night-time lunar landscape with a faint glow. It's just like here on Earth when a bright Moon casts its silvery light on the ground.

Earth's reflected light is brightest in the northern hemisphere's spring.

In 1651, an Italian astronomer named Giovanni Battista Riccioli gave the "seas" their beautiful names.

Sea of Serenity ....

Sea of Crises

Sea of Tranquility ....

Sea of Fecundity

Lunar seas

I f you had been looking up at the Moon a few billion years ago, you would have witnessed one of the most spectacular sights ever to occur in the Solar System. A hail of asteroids pounded into the Moon, gouging out huge holes, called basins, in the surface.

Over time, these enormous scars became filled with molten rock seeping up from the insides of the Moon. Eventually, this cooled and solidified to form vast, open plains — these are the dark grey areas that we can see on the face of the Moon today. Early astronomers thought these areas looked like giant pools of water, so they called them lunar *maria* (the Latin word for seas). This is quite a misleading name, as there aren't any watery waves lapping their shores. Instead, the Moon's surface is covered in fine, powdered rock called regolith.

The lunar seas
are darker and
smoother than their
cratered surroundings.

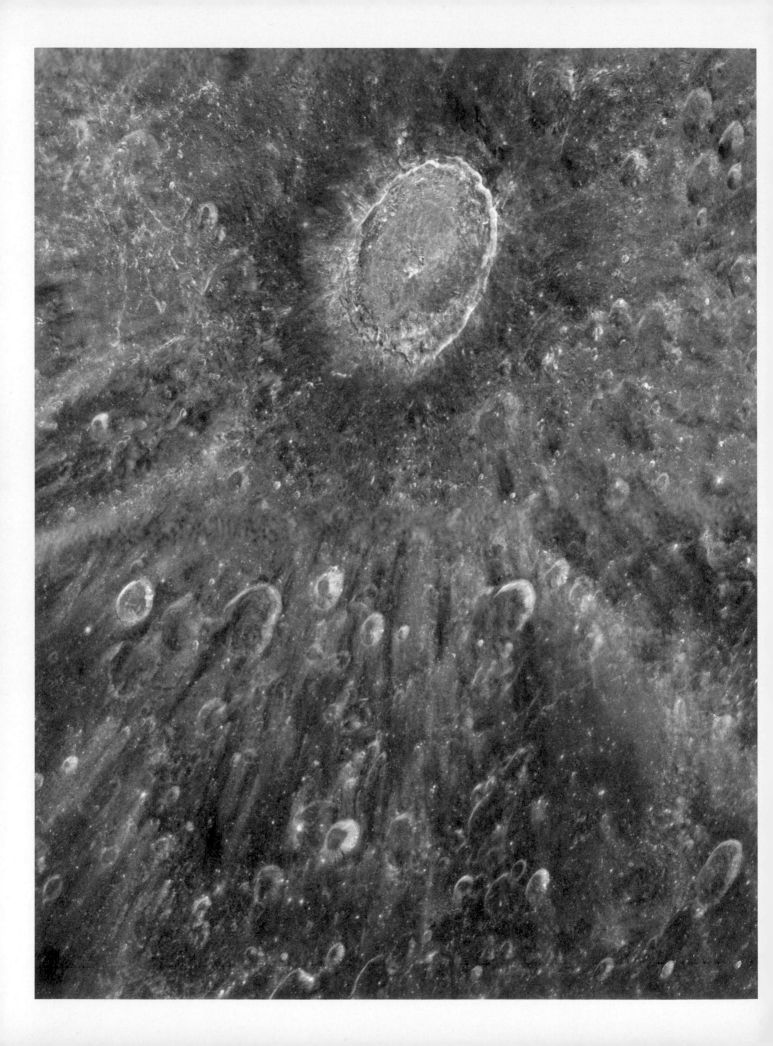

Tycho

Tycho

When the first astronomers to use telescopes turned these newly invented instruments towards the Moon, they were captivated by what they could see. Huge areas of its silvery grey face were covered in enormous dish-shaped pits, creating a rugged and pockmarked landscape. Today, we know that these craters are the result of asteroids and comets crashing into the Moon and gouging out great chunks of its surface.

One of the most impressive lunar craters is Tycho. When it was formed, the impact was so great that part of the Moon's surface bounced back upwards to create mountains in its centre! With a small telescope, you can even see where debris shot away from Tycho as the asteroid crashed into the lunar rock — these are the bright streaks that extend out from the crater.

Tycho is so large that
it could fit all of London
within its walls.

Scientists think Tycho is about 100 million years old — it hasn't yet been damaged by other asteroid impacts.

Moonwalking

So far, only 12 people have walked on the Moon's surface. The first was Neil Armstrong, in 1969.

Imagine what it must feel like to step out onto another world — a place where the sky is pitch black and where there is no air or clouds, so distant landscapes look crisp and clear. A place without trees or plants, where the ground all around is a dark grey powder peppered with craggy rocks and boulders.

This is the scene that faced the astronauts who travelled to the surface of the Moon on the Apollo missions of the late 1960s and early 1970s. As they took these extraordinary first steps, the moonwalkers snapped pictures, carried out experiments, and on some missions even drove a specially built moon buggy. There is no wind or liquid water on the Moon to disturb the landscape, so the astronauts' footprints are preserved in the lunar dust to this day.

Can you spot the astronauts' footprints?

The Sun

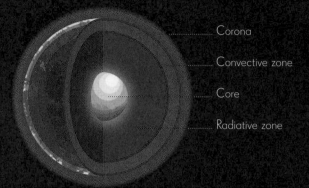

Corona

Convective zone

Core

Radiative zone

Did you know that the Sun is a star, just like the countless points of light sparkling in the night sky? In fact, it is relatively small compared to some of the other stars in the Milky Way. But it's still the object our little planetary family — the Solar System — whirls around, and its warmth and light make the Earth a place where life can exist.

The Sun's power comes from reactions unfolding deep within its core — here, superheated matter is fused, or joined together, under immense temperatures and pressures. This process releases energy, which works its way out from the centre to create the blazing hot, glowing ball that travels across the sky.

Astronomers think the Sun will
live for about another 5 billion years.

Remember: never, ever look directly at the Sun —
it is so bright that it will damage your eyes!

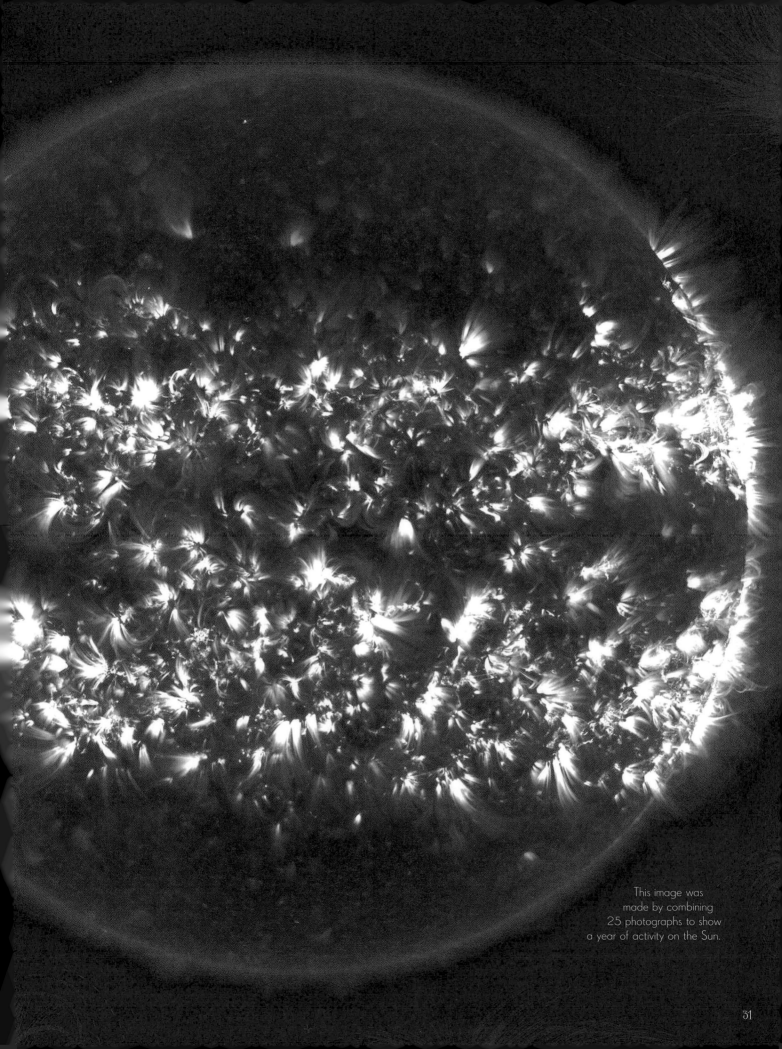

This image was
made by combining
25 photographs to show
a year of activity on the Sun.

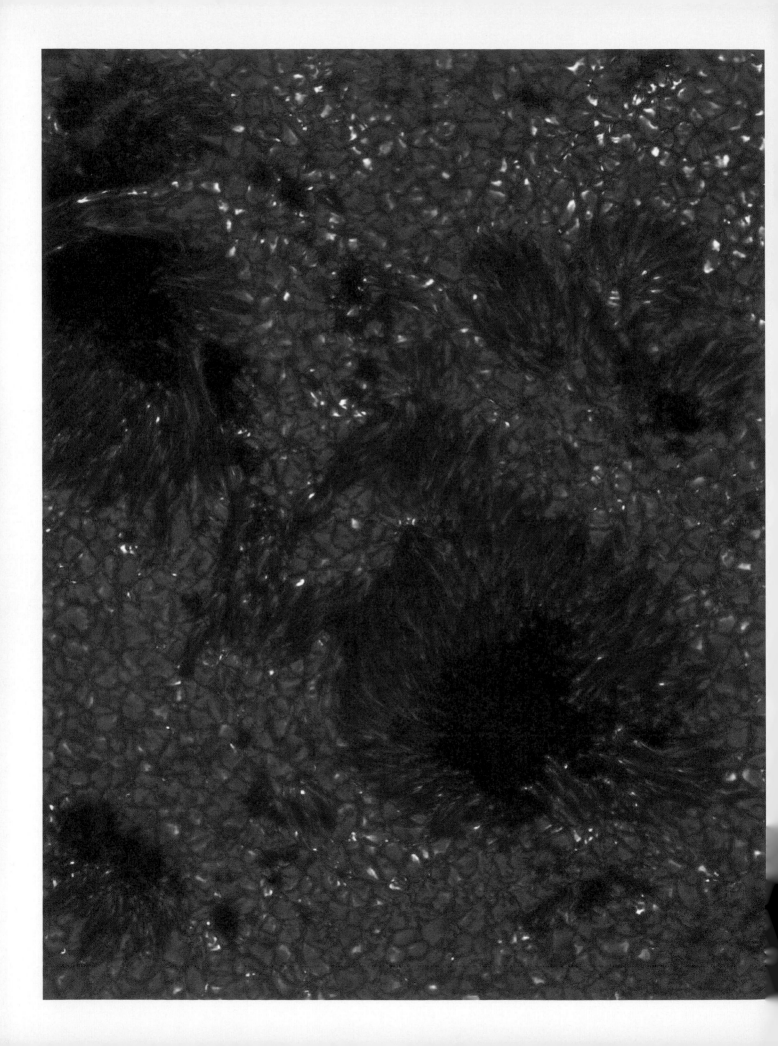

Sunspots

A single sunspot can be bigger than the entire Earth!

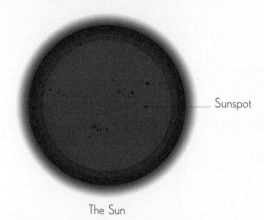

.... Sunspot

The Sun

The surface of the Sun is unlike any other place in the Solar System. It has been bubbling and blazing away every second for billions of years, beaming with incredible amounts of heat and light.

Astronomers call the Sun's surface the photosphere, and it has a temperature of around 5,400 °C (9,752 °F). Sometimes, magnetic fields emerging from inside the Sun reduce the amount of heat reaching parts of the surface. This creates cooler, darker patches of the photosphere, which we call sunspots. Larger sunspots usually have two parts to them — a dark heart, called an umbra, and a lighter border known as a penumbra. Sunspots can last many months, or they can disappear in just a few days.

Sunspots sometimes appear in groups, like these ones spotted by the Swedish Solar Telescope.

Remember, it's important to never look directly at the Sun!

Rain on the Sun

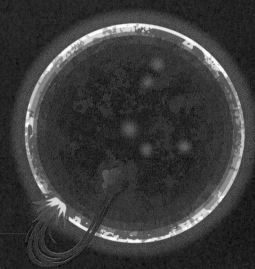

Solar prominence ....

The Sun

From Earth, the Sun is little more than a ball of burning light. But up in space, solar observatories monitoring our star have revealed incredible events taking place on its surface and in its atmosphere.

Every so often, huge arches of what looks like fire start to leap out from the Sun. These can change and move over the course of just minutes. They're known as solar prominences, and they're made of a superheated matter called plasma. As the plasma erupts from the Sun, it can trace the curved lines of looping magnetic fields in the atmosphere before falling back to the solar surface in blazing streams that scientists call coronal rain.

Sometimes the Sun blasts material towards Earth, where it can produce spellbinding auroras.

Plasma leaps up to follow magnetic loops before falling back to the surface.

Total solar eclipse

The white wisps around the Moon during a total solar eclipse are part of the Sun's outer atmosphere, known as the corona.

Sometimes, the shadow of the Moon sweeps across the globe of the Earth. When this happens, anyone standing where the darker, central part of this shadow falls will experience a total solar eclipse. A total solar eclipse usually happens at least once every couple of years.

During these spine-tingling events, the daylight slowly begins to fade to twilight. The air cools, and animals often behave as if they're preparing for the evening. Soon after, a strange, silvery light falls on the landscape, and for a few moments all goes dark, as the Sun is blocked entirely by the black disc of the Moon — this event is known as totality. As the core of the Moon's shadow moves away, totality ends and the Sun's light gradually returns.

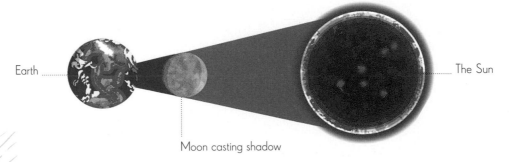

Earth

Moon casting shadow

The Sun

This total solar eclipse took place in 2016 and could be seen from most parts of Indonesia.

Remember, it's important to never look directly at the Sun!

The Solar System

There may be another world orbiting at a
huge distance from the Sun - we just
haven't discovered it yet!

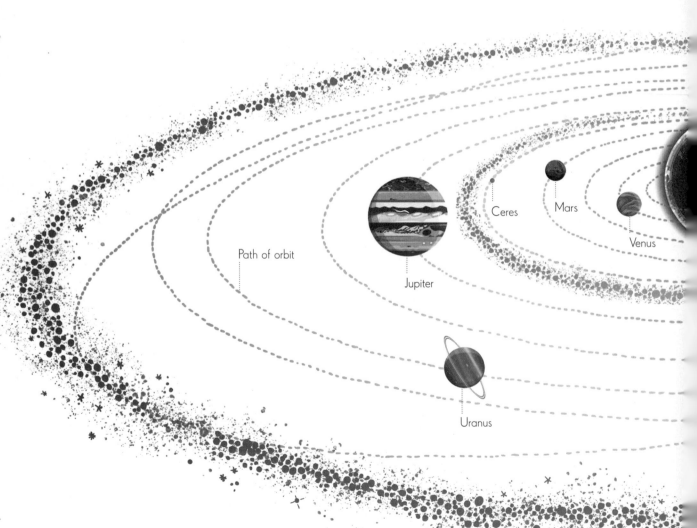

Ceres

Mars

Venus

Path of orbit

Jupiter

Uranus

The Sun sits at the centre of an enormous family of objects that whirl around it as they all move through the Milky Way. Together, this extraordinary collection is known as the Solar System. It includes the eight main planets and their moons, and also a fascinating array of smaller worlds like Pluto and Ceres. It's also home to asteroids and comets — these objects are tiny compared to planets like Earth, but they swarm around the Sun in vast numbers.

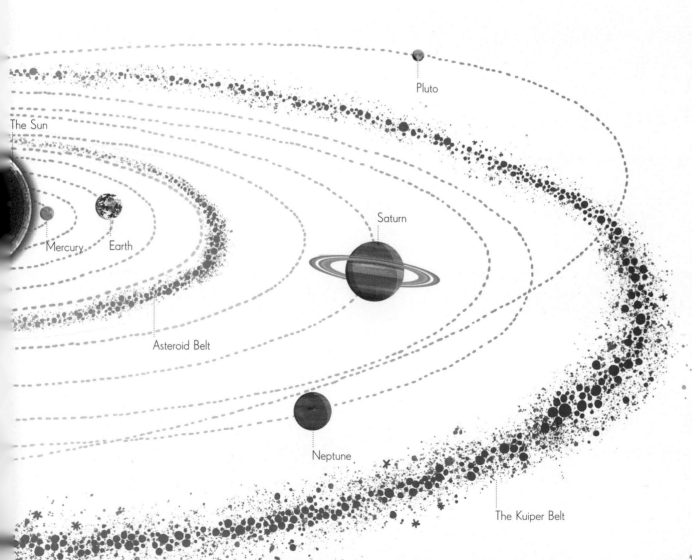

Pluto

The Sun

Mercury Earth

Saturn

Asteroid Belt

Neptune

The Kuiper Belt

Venus

Mercury

The rocky planets

The Sun   • Mercury   ● Venus   🜨 Earth   • Mars

Mercury, Venus, and Mars are close enough to Earth that we can sometimes see them without a telescope.

Earth

Mars

Huddled at the heart of the Solar System are the four inner planets: Mercury, Venus, Earth, and Mars. Like the four larger planets further out, these worlds are thought to have come from an enormous doughnut-shaped disc of dust and gas that encircled the newborn Sun.

One theory says that, over time, small rocks and pebbles began to form within this disc. They collided and stuck to each other, eventually building much larger objects that merged into worlds. The inner planets are small and mostly made of rock and metal. Scientists think this is because the icy ingredients that helped make the distant gas giants couldn't have survived this close to the heat of the young Sun.

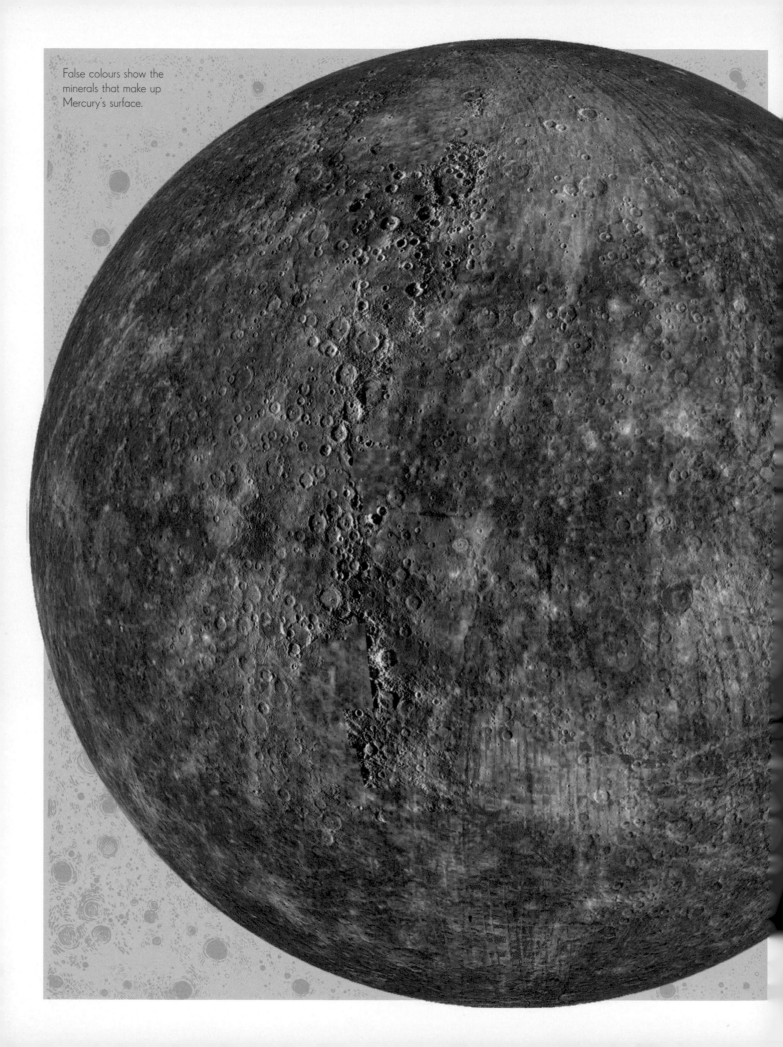

False colours show the minerals that make up Mercury's surface.

At 4,879 km (3,032 miles) across, Mercury is
the smallest planet in the Solar System.

Mercury

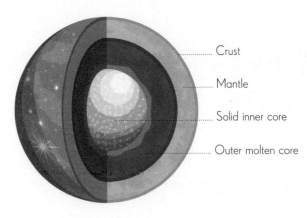

Crust

Mantle

Solid inner core

Outer molten core

Inside Mercury

The planet Mercury is named after the quick-footed
messenger of the Roman gods, which is fitting since it
races around the Sun, taking just 88 days to complete its orbit.
Mercury is the closest planet to the Sun, and its surface
temperature can reach a blistering 430 °C (806 °F).

Its rocky crust shows the scars of asteroid and comet impacts, with
almost its entire globe covered in craters. Yet Mercury holds surprises
too. In its polar regions, there are places — at the bottom of deep
craters — that the blazing sunlight cannot reach. There might be
water ice lurking in these tucked-away shaded spots.

The transit of Mercury

As the inner planets, Mercury and Venus, whirl around the Sun, they sometimes swoop in front of its face, from the perspective of Earth. These events are quite rare, and they're called transits. The last transit of Mercury occurred back in 2019 and the next one will happen in the year 2032.

Professional astronomers use transits to discover worlds orbiting other stars far from our own Solar System. They do this by using special space telescopes to record the brightness of these distant stars. If a star dims briefly, it may be a sign that a transit has occurred — that is, a planet has passed in front of the star and blocked a tiny bit of its light.

Remember, it's important to never look directly at the Sun!

In 1629 a German astronomer called
Johannes Kepler became the first
person to predict a transit of Mercury.

The impact that made the Caloris Basin
was so violent it may have created
hills on the opposite side of Mercury.

Caloris Basin

Caloris Basin ....

Let's imagine you're a scientist trying to understand the amazing landscape in this picture of Mercury's surface. What do you think caused that huge, circular feature at the centre? And were most of those smaller craters inside the circle formed before or after it?

If you said this feature was made by an object — such as a massive asteroid — crashing into Mercury, you're absolutely right! That enormous ring is known as the Caloris Basin, and it is larger than the size of France. The smaller craters are on top of the features of the Caloris Basin, so they must have formed after it was made. This is the kind of detective work scientists do all the time to uncover the secrets of the Solar System.

The Caloris Basin
is peppered with
hundreds of
smaller craters

Venus

Venus is the second brightest natural
object in our night sky, after the Moon.

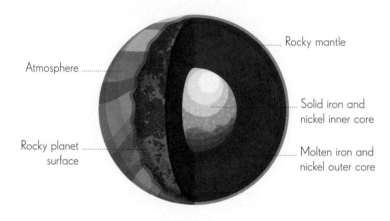

Atmosphere ....

Rocky mantle

.... Solid iron and
nickel inner core

Rocky planet ....
surface

.... Molten iron and
nickel outer core

Inside Venus

Even though it can float up to 261 million km (162 million miles) away from Earth, Venus is still one of our closest planetary neighbours. The two planets are almost the same size, so they are sometimes called twins, but their stories are very different.

Some scientists think that in the distant past, Venus had oceans of liquid water. However, these have long since disappeared, and today all that remains is a volcanic landscape blanketed by thick clouds. What little we do know about the surface of Venus has come largely from a handful of space probes that have visited the planet. Some of these actually travelled down to the surface, where they experienced roasting temperatures of 460 °C (860 °F) and crushing pressure from the toxic atmosphere.

Below the clouds,
scientists think Venus
looks something like this.

One of the tallest volcanoes on Venus is called
Maat Mons, after the Egyptian goddess of truth, Ma'at.

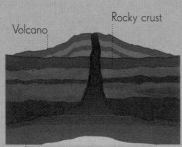

Volcano

Rocky crust

Magma chamber

Volcanoes on Venus

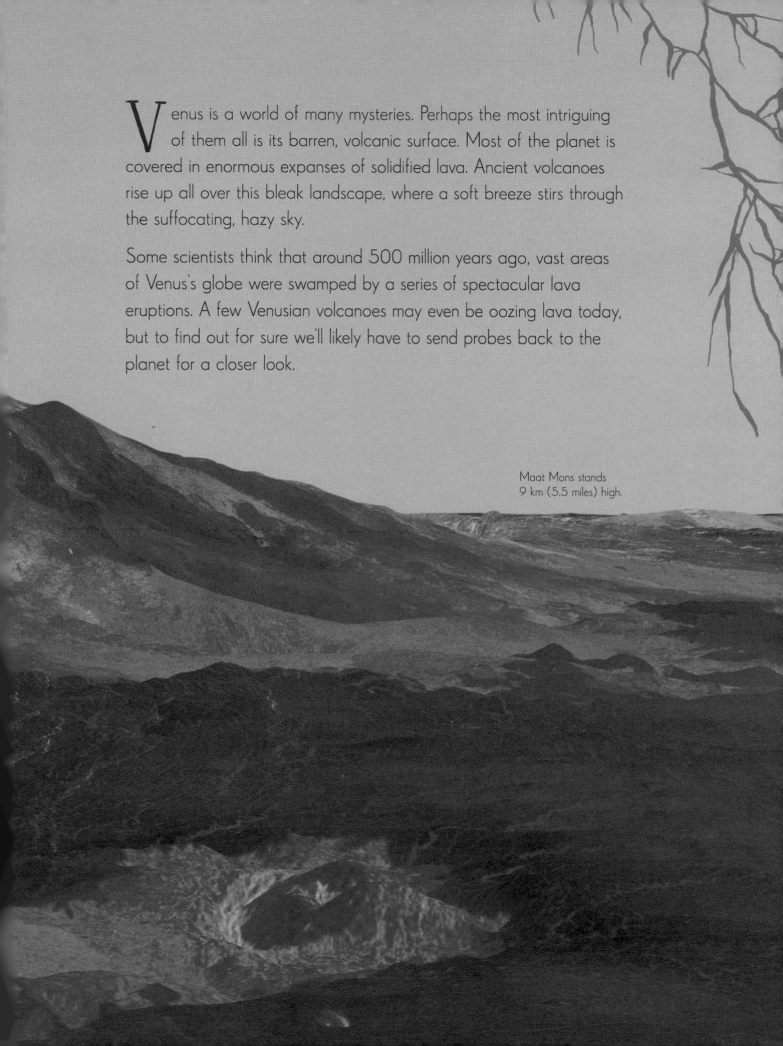

Venus is a world of many mysteries. Perhaps the most intriguing of them all is its barren, volcanic surface. Most of the planet is covered in enormous expanses of solidified lava. Ancient volcanoes rise up all over this bleak landscape, where a soft breeze stirs through the suffocating, hazy sky.

Some scientists think that around 500 million years ago, vast areas of Venus's globe were swamped by a series of spectacular lava eruptions. A few Venusian volcanoes may even be oozing lava today, but to find out for sure we'll likely have to send probes back to the planet for a closer look.

Maat Mons stands
9 km (5.5 miles) high.

Venus is named after the
Roman goddess of love.

Deadly clouds

Sometimes Venus can appear in the dark sky as a dazzling point of light — one that easily outshines the other planets. What gives it this stunning sparkling quality? The answer lies in this picture: Venus's cloud tops are a bright, yellowish-white.

Images from spacecraft that have visited the planet show enormous, billowing cloud patterns stretching right across the Venusian globe. Though these clouds may be pretty, they are laced with sulphuric acid, and they float in a thick, choking atmosphere rich with carbon dioxide. The top layers rain droplets of acid that evaporate before they hit the ground.

The clouds of Venus
trap heat, making it
the hottest planet in
our Solar System.

Mars

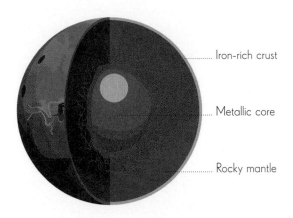

Iron-rich crust

Metallic core

Rocky mantle

Inside Mars

As we travel away from the Sun, we cross the path of a world that humans may one day visit: Mars. For centuries, humans have looked toward this little world and imagined what wonders might lie there. Today, we know more about the "Red Planet" than ever before.

As you read this right now, there's a good chance a rover or lander is exploring some part of the sandy, rocky surface of Mars, while spacecraft with cameras whirl above, snapping dramatic shots. We now know this is a planet covered in windswept plains, and scarred by vast canyons and enormous volcanic peaks. But the rocks and valleys of Mars also tell us that it wasn't always so desolate and dusty. Could life once have existed here?

Mars is named after the ancient Roman god of war, because its reddish colour made people think of blood!

Valles Marineris

When astronauts travel to Mars in the future, one of the most spectacular features they'll see will be the Valles Marineris, or Mariner Valley. This immense canyon is a deep, roughly straight, gouge in the Martian surface that stretches an astonishing 2,200 km (1,367 miles) across the planet — longer than the entire length of Italy! Even today, the great mystery of the Valles Marineris is how it formed. Scientists have several ideas. For example, some believe the Martian crust split and a wide swathe slumped downwards.

Valles Marineris

The Grand Canyon

The walls of the Valles Marineris drop a hair-raising 10 km (6.2 miles) in some places. Earth's Grand Canyon looks tiny in comparison!

The Valles Marineris looks like a huge scar on the planet's surface.

Olympus Mons

Olympus Mons may look flat from
a distance, but it's actually more than
twice the height of Mount Everest.

Olympus Mons

When it comes to spectacular volcanoes, Mars takes the top spot. The mighty Olympus Mons is a shield volcano, which means it has a very broad base, with gently sloping sides. It's much larger than any volcano on Earth. From its base to its peak, it gradually rises a staggering 21.9 km (13.6 miles) into the Martian sky, while its sides span about 640 km (398 miles) — it would take a jet airliner more than 40 minutes to fly across it. It is thought that Olympus Mons formed around 3.6 billion years ago, when huge amounts of lava oozed from the insides of the Red Planet.

The pit at the top of
Olympus Mons is about
the size of Luxembourg!

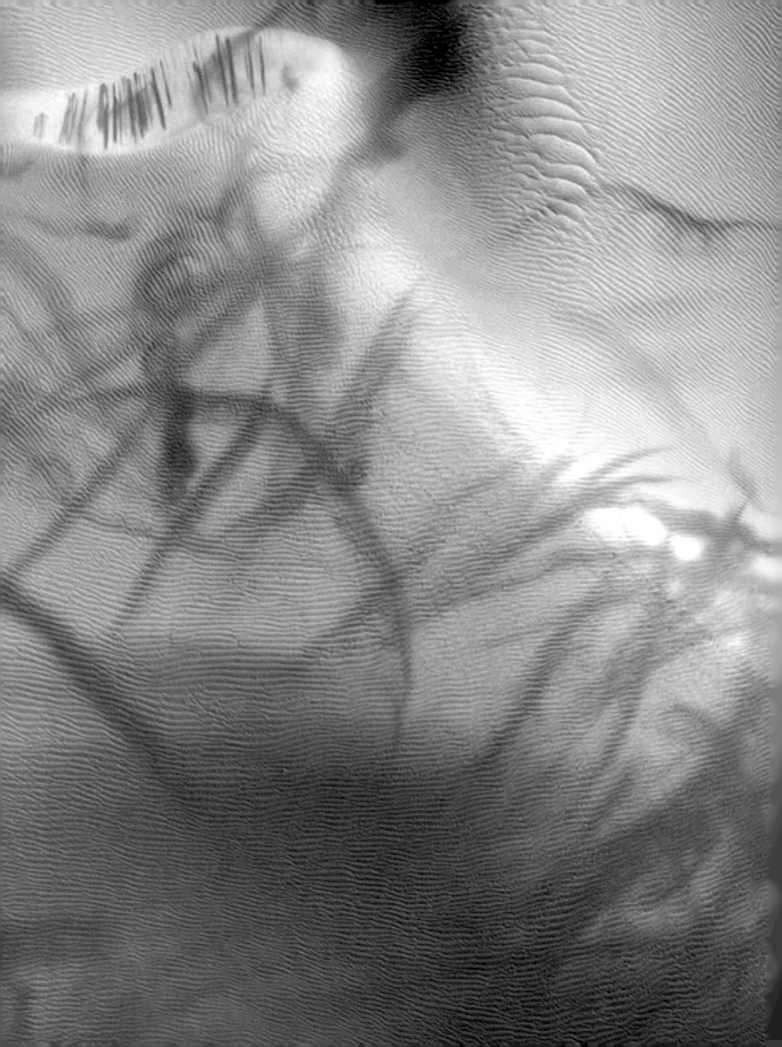

Martian dust devils

Look at these strange tracks on Mars's surface. It looks as if somebody has been scribbling in the Martian dust. In fact, it wasn't somebody, but something. Dust devils — spinning vortexes of air like little tornadoes — have whipped over the ground, leaving trails that record their path.

Several spacecraft have caught these whirlwinds in the act of flitting across the Red Planet. We now know there are other dusty phenomena in Mars's skies, too: enormous dust storms occasionally stir within the planet's atmosphere, enshrouding its globe in a murky, brown haze.

The wind on Mars has helped clean dust from the solar panels of rovers exploring the planet!

Dust devils leave dark marks on Mars's dusty surface.

Water on Mars

This image looks down on an ancient Martian river valley called Nirgal Vallis.

If you could somehow walk safely across Mars today, you'd probably only hear the sound of a soft breeze stirring across the landscape, or the occasional flurry of an enormous dust storm. Billions of years ago, however, you may also have been able to listen out for the crashing of waves and the roar of a river carving its way through the Martian rock.

We think this because scientists have found clues, all over Mars, revealing how its surface was sculpted by large amounts of liquid water. Orbiting spacecraft have captured pictures of dried-up river valleys and lakes, while on the ground, rovers have found rocks and minerals that must have formed in a watery environment.

This is what Mars might have looked like many years ago!

Mars may have once had a large ocean in its northern hemisphere.

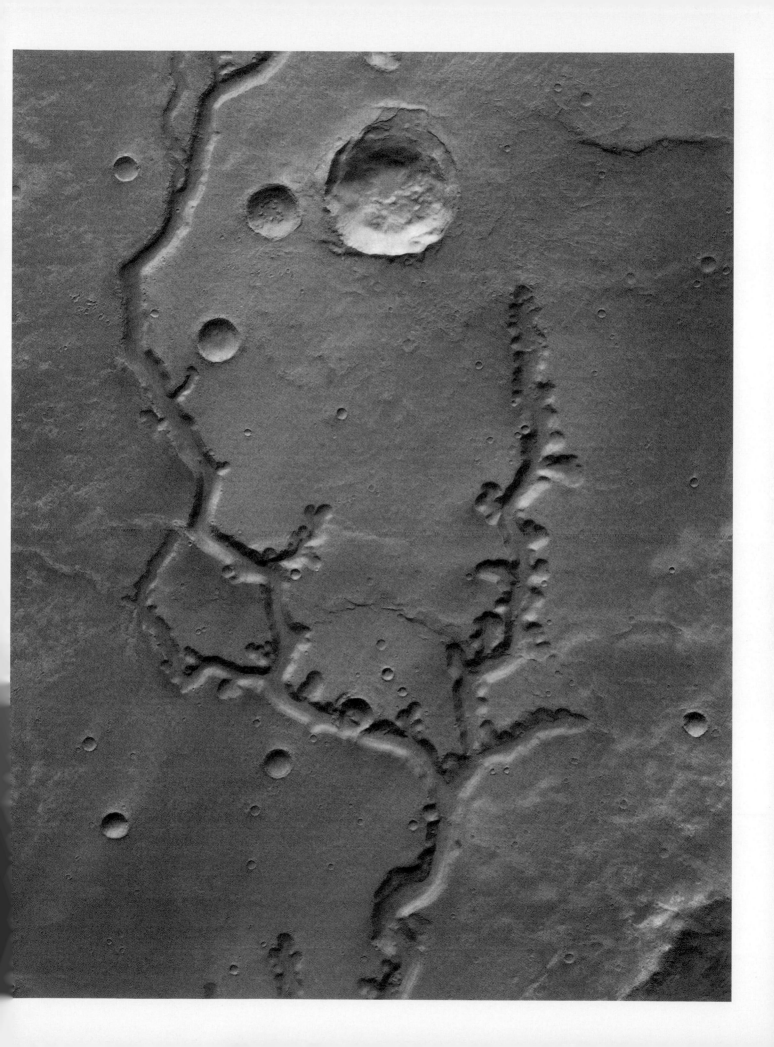

Exploring Mars

Mars's colour comes from iron oxide in its soil — the same stuff that makes rust orangey-red.

The first humans to visit Mars might think it looks a little like home. Landscapes of rocky hills and craggy mountains loom over the brownish-red soil, while elsewhere valleys cut through desert-like plains and huge fields of sand dunes stretch to the horizon.

Under the hazy sky, though, these early explorers will soon see how different the Red Planet is to Earth. They will need protection from the Sun's harsh ultraviolet light, and they'll have to trek across uneven terrain — Mars is peppered with craters, small and large. NASA's Curiosity rover has been roaming the planet for years, examining its atmosphere and geology. Future robotic missions will dig deep below the Martian surface to see if conditions there could support life.

The Curiosity rover landed on Mars in 2012 to find out about conditions on the planet.

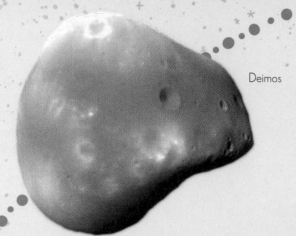

Deimos

Phobos and Deimos are named after the horses that pulled the Roman god of war's chariot.

The moons of Mars

Mars has two moons, called Phobos and Deimos. At roughly 23 km (14 miles) in diameter, Phobos is the larger of the two — Deimos is about 12 km (7.5 miles) across. Scientists are not sure where these moons came from. They could be space rocks that were captured by Mars's gravity, or debris from a gigantic asteroid impact on the Martian surface long ago. The moons are oddly shaped and lumpy — this is because they aren't massive enough for their own gravity to squish them into a ball, like other, larger moons in the Solar System.

As it orbits around Mars, Phobos is, very slowly, moving towards the planet. In just over 30 million years, it may even fall onto the Martian surface. Imagine seeing that!

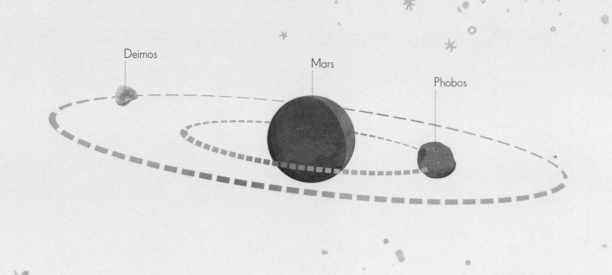

Deimos

Mars

Phobos

Phobos

Vesta

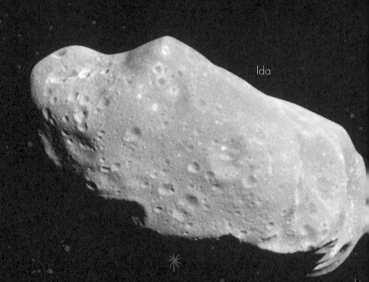

Ida

Asteroids

Did you know that the Solar System swarms with thousands upon thousands of lumpy objects called asteroids? Asteroids are the materials that were left over after the planets had finished forming. Some are quite rocky, while others are thought to be made of different kinds of metal. Many of the asteroids in our Solar System lie in a huge ring between Mars and Jupiter called the asteroid belt, but there are many others scattered all over, and probably more out there that we've yet to spot!

Eros

The asteroid belt

Bennu

NASA has sent a spacecraft
to take a sample from the
asteroid Bennu and bring
it back to Earth.

Ceres

Ceres is one of five dwarf
planets in our Solar System.

Icy crust ....

Slushy salt water

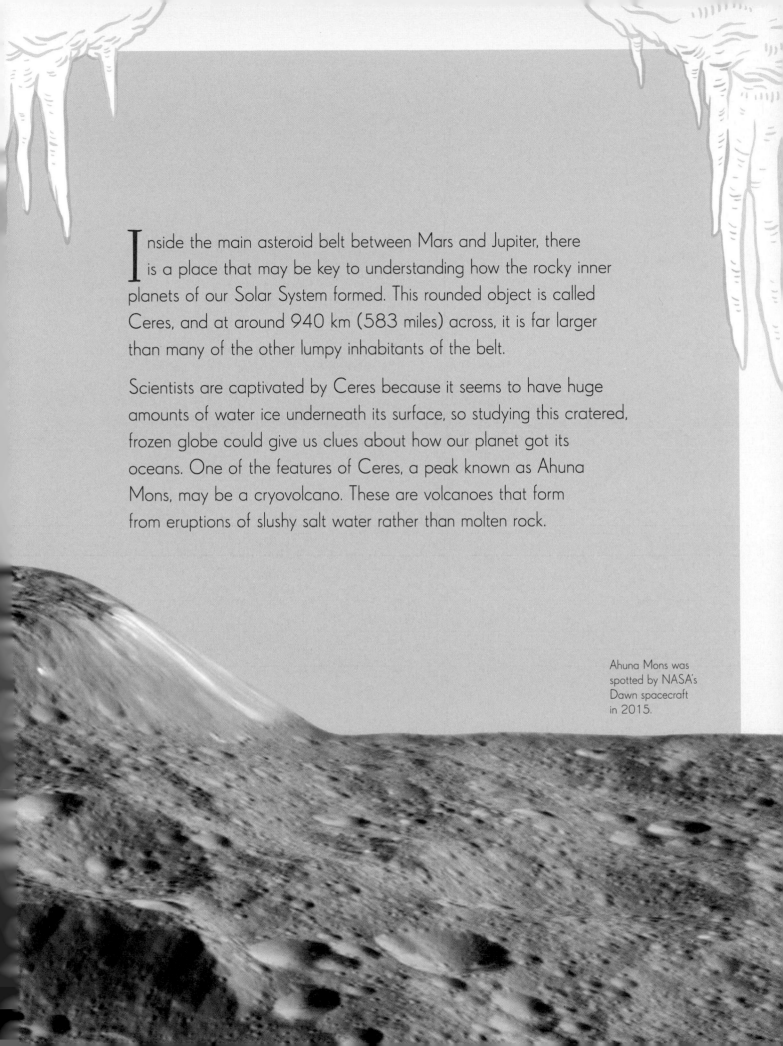

Inside the main asteroid belt between Mars and Jupiter, there is a place that may be key to understanding how the rocky inner planets of our Solar System formed. This rounded object is called Ceres, and at around 940 km (583 miles) across, it is far larger than many of the other lumpy inhabitants of the belt.

Scientists are captivated by Ceres because it seems to have huge amounts of water ice underneath its surface, so studying this cratered, frozen globe could give us clues about how our planet got its oceans. One of the features of Ceres, a peak known as Ahuna Mons, may be a cryovolcano. These are volcanoes that form from eruptions of slushy salt water rather than molten rock.

Ahuna Mons was spotted by NASA's Dawn spacecraft in 2015.

Jupiter

The gas giants

Beyond the rubble of the asteroid belt is the realm of the giant planets in our Solar System — Jupiter, Saturn, Uranus, and Neptune. These four worlds, with their thick atmospheres made up of gases such as hydrogen and helium, are spread out over vast distances. Some scientists think that billions of years ago the gas giants jostled around within the Solar System. As this happened, their orbits around the Sun moved, and some may have even swapped places! These dramatic changes scattered asteroids and other small objects in different directions. What was left is the planetary neighbourhood we can spot through telescopes today.

The Sun

The rocky planets

Jupiter

Saturn

Uranus

Neptune

Saturn

Uranus

The smallest gas giant is Neptune - and it's still almost four times larger than Earth.

Neptune

The shape of a dolphin lurks
in Jupiter's cloud patterns.
Can you spot it?

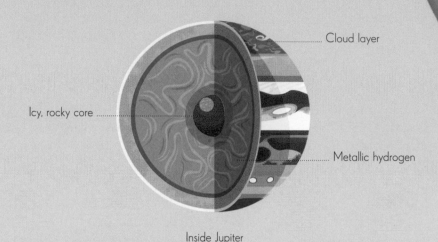

Cloud layer

Icy, rocky core

Metallic hydrogen

Inside Jupiter

Io

Jupiter

Jupiter is the largest world in our Solar System — so big that it could fit just over 11 Earths across its face. This tremendous size means that, despite it being far away from our planet, we can sometimes see it in the night sky as a shining point of light.

If you look really carefully, using a good pair of binoculars, you might be able to spot Jupiter's four largest moons — Io, Europa, Ganymede, and Callisto. The moons will look like little star-like specks close to the bright planet. As these moons travel around Jupiter they change position night by night, so occasionally all four aren't visible from Earth at the same time. Today, we know there are at least 79 moons in total orbiting Jupiter — but there may be other tiny ones that nobody has spotted yet!

Jupiter's day is only 10 hours long.
It spins so quickly that its
middle bulges outwards!

Jupiter's atmosphere is mostly made up
of hydrogen and helium, but it also contains
other gases like smelly ammonia.

Swirling clouds

If you could fly above Jupiter and look down on its clouds, this is the sort of view you would have. Huge swirls and pastel-coloured ripples would stretch into the distance as far as the eyes could see. Some clouds would tower so high they would cast massive shadows onto the cloud layers below them. And if you watched for long enough, you'd see that the planet's entire atmosphere is flowing and churning.

If your imaginary spacecraft zoomed higher, you'd notice that Jupiter's globe is stripey — astronomers call the lightly coloured atmospheric bands "zones" and the darker parts "belts".

Zone

Belt

This coloured image
shows the clouds
of Jupiter in its
northern hemisphere.

Stormy planet

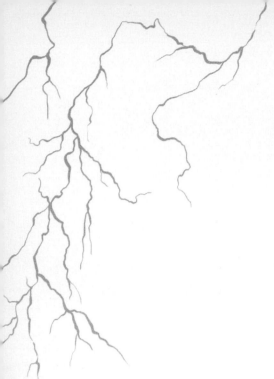

Jupiter is named after the Roman king of the gods.
He was also the god of the sky and thunder.

Jupiter's thick atmosphere is home to countless violent, swirling storms. They come in all sizes, from small ones that form and die quickly, to huge, spinning spots that can last for months and even years! The biggest storm on Jupiter is also the most famous in all the Solar System. It is called the Great Red Spot, and for good reason — it's bigger than Earth, and its whirling orangey-red clouds have been raging for over 180 years, possibly even longer!

Over the years, the
Great Red Spot has
varied in size and shape

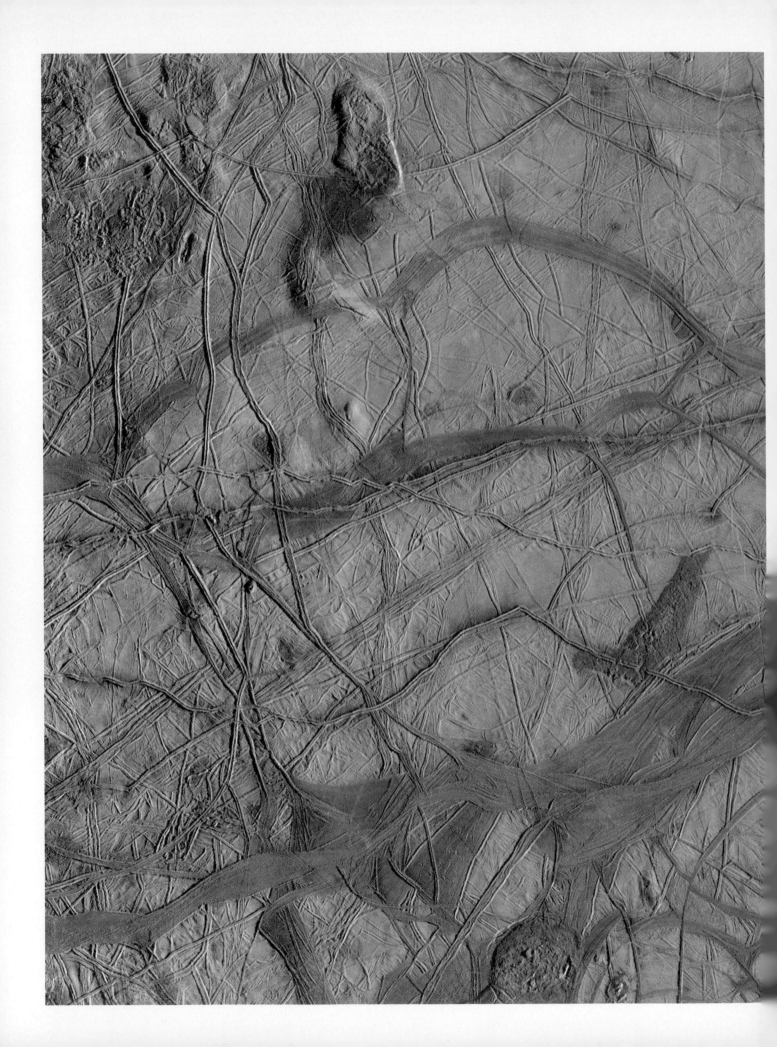

Europa

In some places, the ice that makes Europa's crust could be thicker than Earth's deepest ocean!

Jupiter's moon Europa is a fascinating place. It was first spotted by the Italian stargazer Galileo Galilei in 1610, so is known as one of the four "Galilean" moons. It is covered by a thick, icy crust that has relatively few craters on it. Huge fissures and giant cracks stretch all across its frozen surface, and it has strange red-brown markings that scientists still don't fully understand.

Under Europa's fractured crust it is thought that there is a layer of liquid water. For this reason, astrobiologists — people who study whether, and how, life might exist on other worlds — are intrigued by this captivating moon. Could anything be living in this dark and distant ocean beneath the ice?

This picture shows Europa's cracked surface.

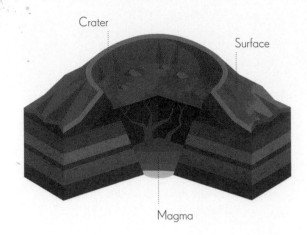

Crater

Surface

Magma

Io and its volcanoes

Can you imagine walking across the landscape on Jupiter's moon Io? It wouldn't be a particularly fun experience. Io's extraordinary bright yellow colour comes from a smelly, toxic chemical called sulphur. It's produced by the incredible amount of volcanic activity on this little world.

You see, Io is a moon that's pockmarked by many volcanoes — some of which are probably active and erupting right now. From the spacecraft that have visited Jupiter and its family of moons, we know there are seething pits of lava bubbling away on Io's surface, and huge volcanic eruptions blasting fountains of sulphurous gases high up into space. If you're ever planning a trip around the Solar System, Io is definitely a place to avoid!

The Galileo spacecraft has spotted
signs of over 100 volcanoes on Io.

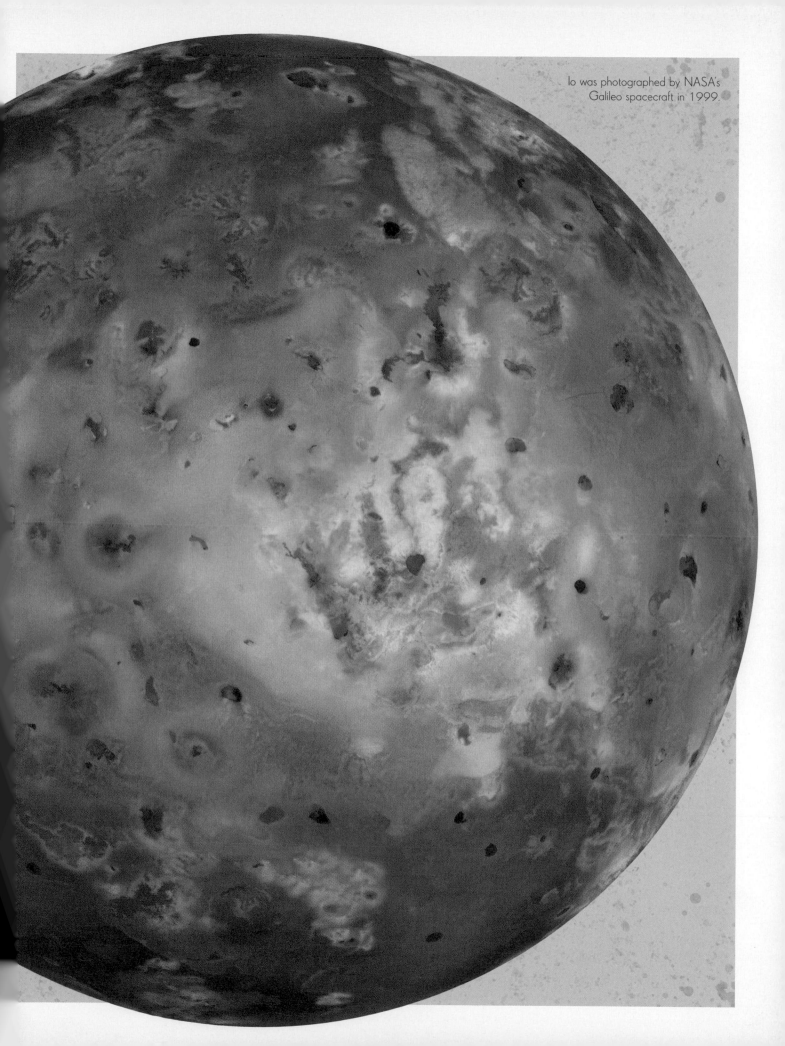

Callisto and Ganymede

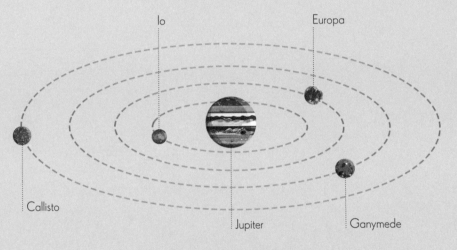

Jupiter and its four largest moons

Callisto and Ganymede are two of the largest moons in the Solar System. In fact, Ganymede is bigger than the planet Mercury! Like many of the objects in our planetary neighbourhood, these moons are dotted with craters. Although they might look like spheres of rock at first glance, they both actually have cold, icy surfaces.

Scientists are planning to send a spacecraft to Jupiter to study these worlds in 2022. This mission may uncover some of the secrets of what Ganymede and Callisto are made of, and what lies beneath their frozen exteriors. This could tell us if these moons, and others like them, have places where life may be able to exist. The mission is called JUICE – or JUpiter ICy moons Explorer!

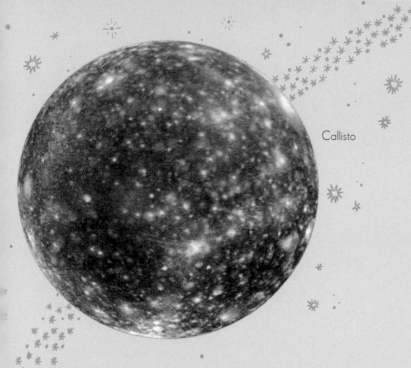

Callisto

Callisto and Ganymede
may have liquid water
oceans hidden deep
below their surfaces.

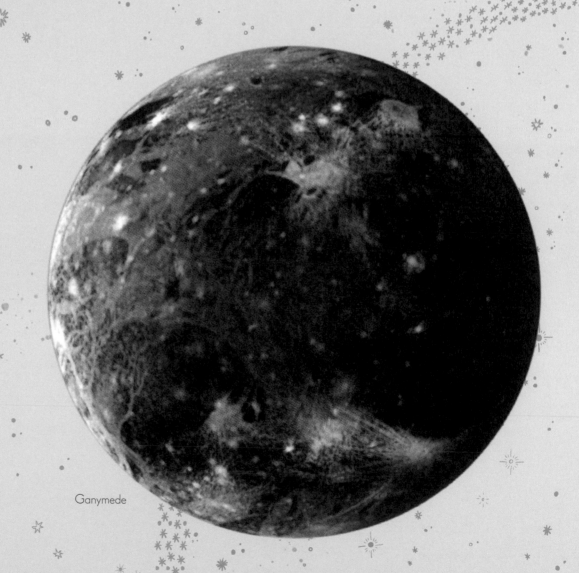

Ganymede

.... Enceladus

.... Tethys

Hydrogen and
helium gas

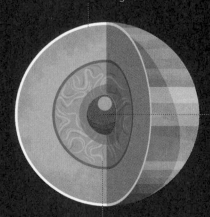

Rock and ice core

Like Earth, both Saturn
and Jupiter have auroras
in their polar regions.

Metallic hydrogen

Inside Saturn

Saturn

Encircled by an exquisite system of rings, Saturn is the second largest planet in our Solar System — just like its neighbour, Jupiter, it's a giant world made mostly of gas, perhaps with an icy and rocky core. Even though Saturn is very large, it isn't very dense — if it were possible to build a swimming pool big enough, Saturn would float in it!

Saturn has 82 moons, making it the planet with the largest known family of moons in the Solar System. Some of its moons are large and spherical, such as Enceladus (see p. 94), and some are small potato-shaped objects that dance gracefully near the edges of the rings. Others have very strange forms indeed, such as Hyperion, which looks like a puffy sponge!

Some of Saturn's moons sculpt the path
of its rings, pushing them into place
with the force of their gravity.

Rings of ice

If a fragment of Saturn's magnificent ring system was floating in front of you right now, it would look similar to a clump of snow. Astronomers aren't sure exactly how all these icy chunks ended up circling Saturn. One idea is that they are the remains of a roving moon that was crumbled into pieces by the twisting and pulling force of the giant planet's gravity. The clumps range in size from tiny particles to boulders about the size of a tennis court!

If you could get up close, you would see that the rings are made of lots of individual streams. Some seem tightly packed together, while others have large gaps between them. Though the main group of rings around Saturn measures about 280,000 km (174,000 miles) across, they're actually incredibly thin — some are only about 10 metres (33 feet) deep.

Saturn's rings almost disappear from view when seen side-on.

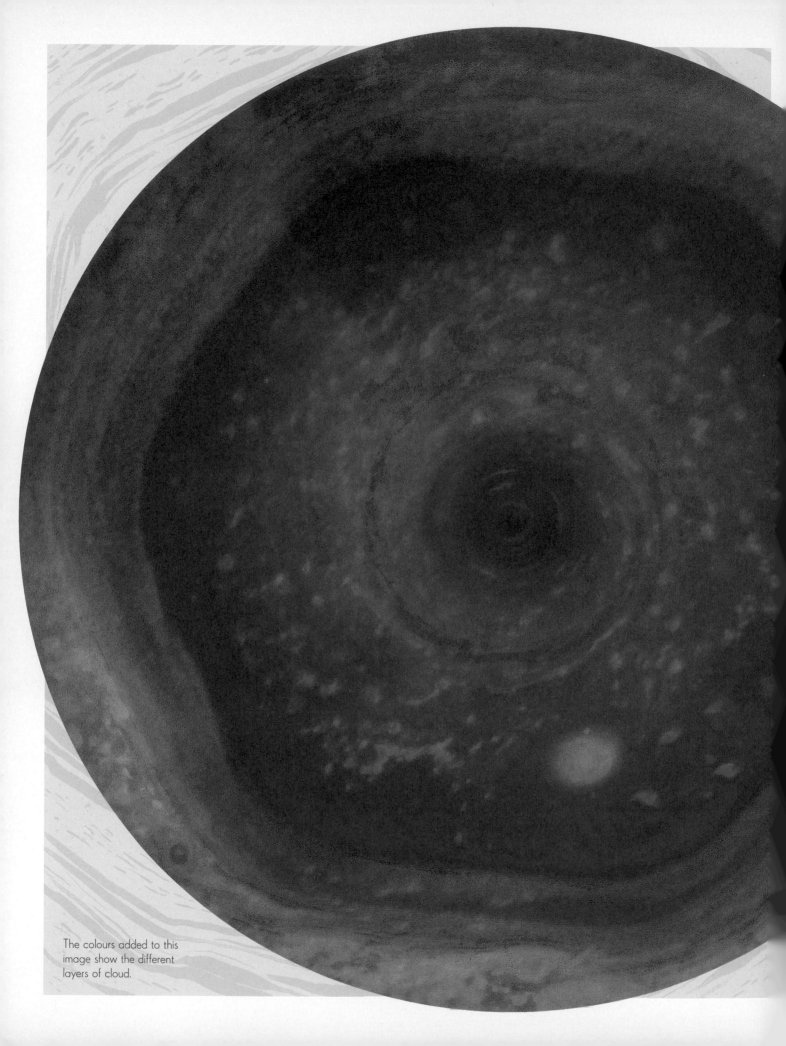

The colours added to this image show the different layers of cloud.

Saturn's polar hexagon

There is a hurricane at the centre of Saturn's polar hexagon.

At the very top of Saturn, above its north pole, lies a spectacular shape. It is a pattern of clouds called a polar hexagon — can you see its six sides?

Scientists think that this strange phenomenon is caused by an atmospheric wave. As the clouds move through Saturn's polar skies, this wave guides their flow, a bit like the way a curving riverbed influences the direction of the water above it. Close-up images of the very heart of the six-sided swirl show towering storm clouds spiralling around inside this unusual maelstrom.

You could fit Earth, the Moon, and Mars side by side within Saturn's polar hexagon - with room to spare!

Titan

The largest sea on Titan,
Kraken Mare, is named after
a mythical sea monster.

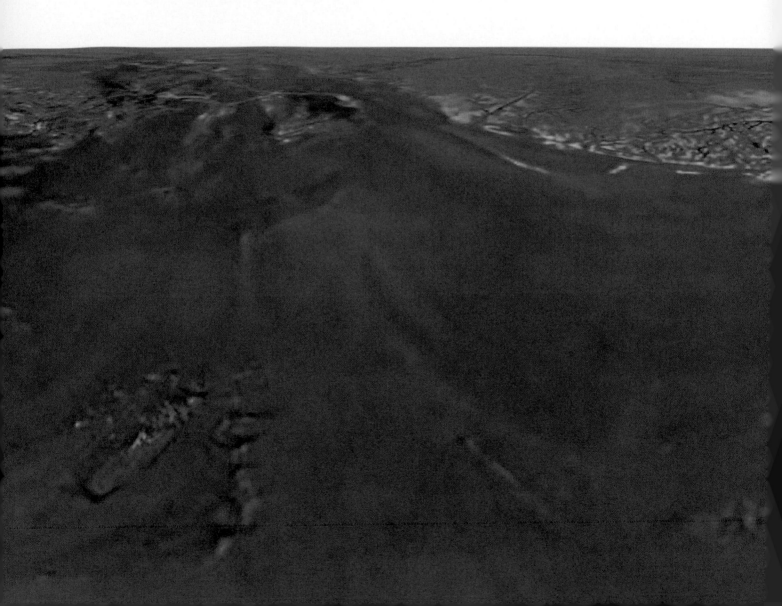

Titan is Saturn's largest moon. It has a thick atmosphere, made mostly of nitrogen, which hides its surface from view. Below the haze lies a frozen landscape of hills, valleys, and wide open plains.

On Earth, ethane and methane are usually found in the form of gas, but on Titan the temperatures are so low that these chemicals form as liquid on the surface, and pool into enormous lakes. This liquid is probably responsible for carving out the winding features that look like river channels, which were spotted by the Cassini spacecraft. In 2005, the Huygens probe landed on Titan and sent back pictures of pebbles of ice scattered across its surface.

Titan's surface is rippled with ridges and valleys.

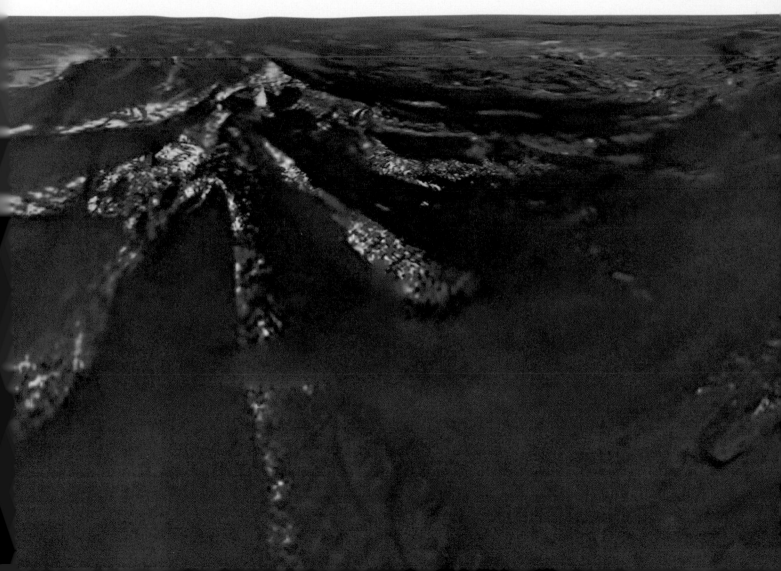

Enceladus

Enceladus is a white world that looks as if a troupe of giant rollerbladers has danced all over it. But it's not just a pretty moon — conditions on Enceladus have made scientists very excited as they try to work out whether life could exist anywhere else in the Solar System.

Scientists believe that under the moon's wrinkly surface of ice there is an ocean of liquid water. Its sea floor may even be home to hydrothermal vents, where warm water swirls through the rocks. But that's not even the most exciting thing about this distant little moon — as the Cassini spacecraft swooped around Saturn, it spotted huge fountains of icy material shooting out of giant fissures in Enceladus's frozen crust. Could these discoveries mean this moon could support life? We don't know — and we may have to travel there to find out…

The icy grains erupting from
Enceladus's fountains form a misty
ring around Saturn called the E ring.

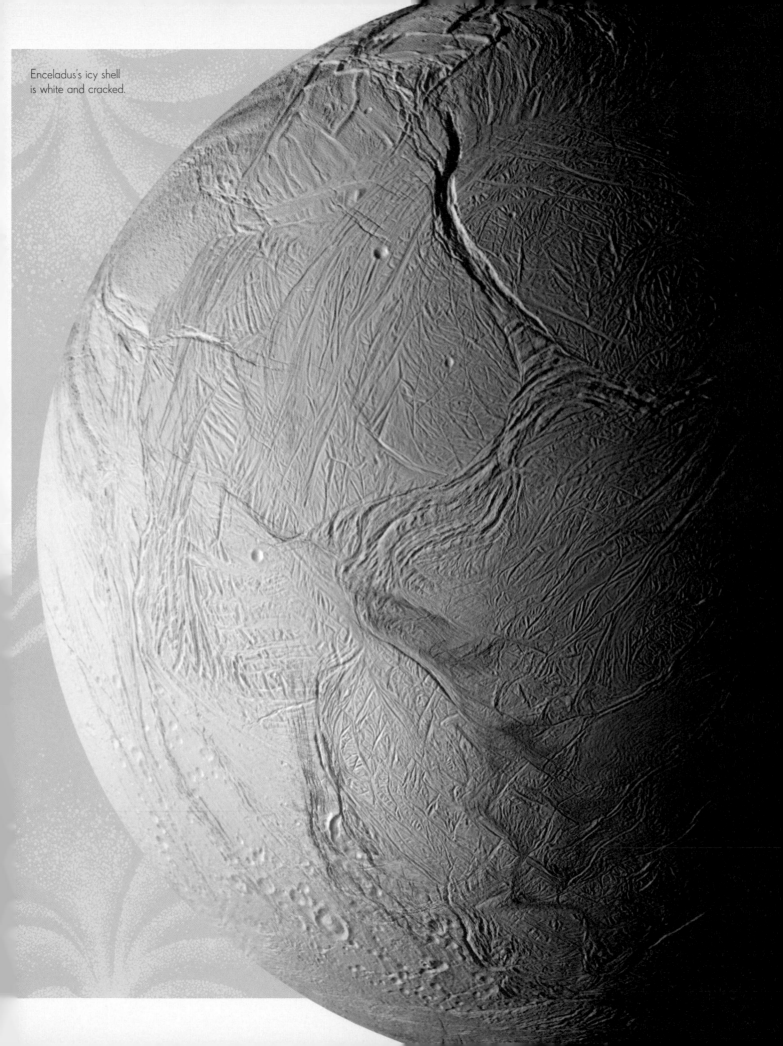

Enceladus's icy shell
is white and cracked.

Iapetus travels around
Saturn at a distance of over
3.5 million km (2.2 million miles)
- that's more than nine times
the distance between the Earth
and the Moon.

Can you spot this
moon's bumpy ridge
peeking out at
the side?

Iapetus

.... Ridge

What do you think could have caused the dark splodges all over the surface of this Saturnian moon, known as Iapteus? If you said they were splats of mud, you're not far from the truth! Scientists think this is dusty material that has fallen onto Iapetus after being blasted off another moon orbiting Saturn, called Phoebe.

Can you see another strange feature of this moon? Around the middle of Iapetus you might spot the unusual ridge that runs part of the way around its equator. It's a mystery how this row of mountains came about — it could have popped up if the moon squished together after it formed, or if Iapetus was spinning around really fast at some point. It might even be the result of space rocks collecting on the surface!

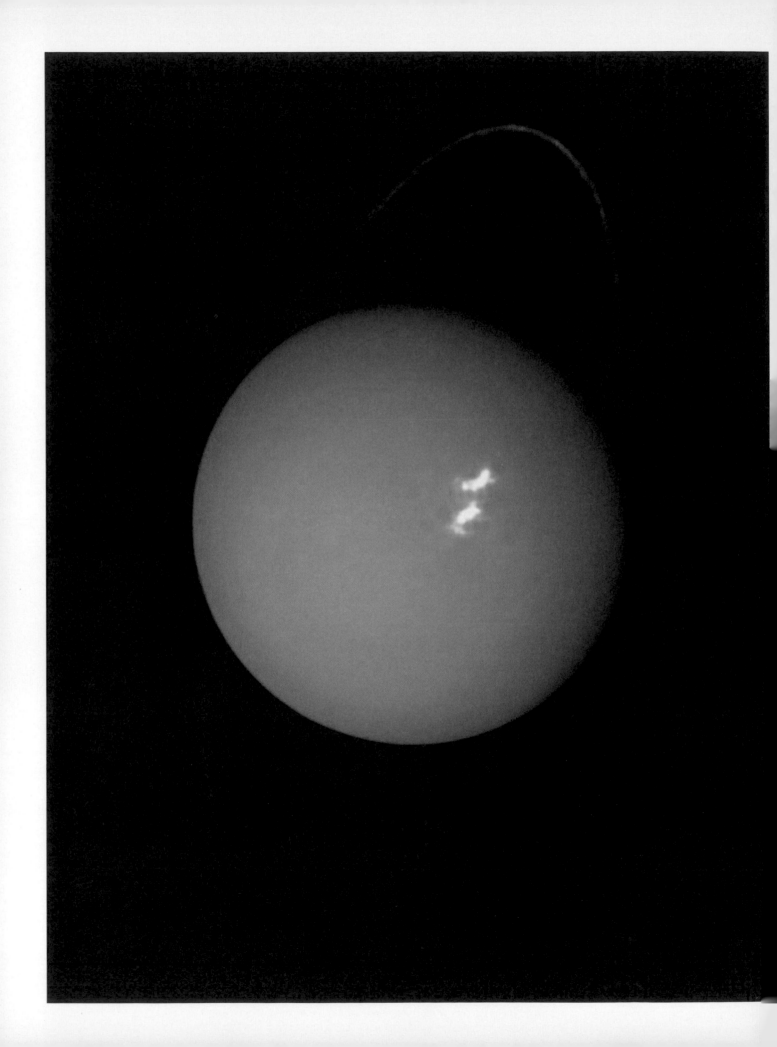

Uranus has five major moons. Its largest,
Miranda, is famous for its huge cliffs -
they're several kilometres high.

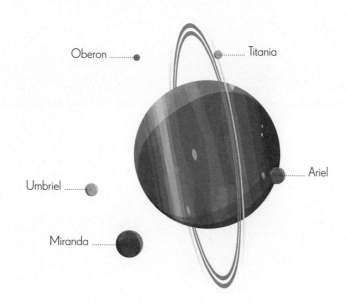

Oberon .... Titania

Umbriel ....

.... Ariel

Miranda ....

Uranus

Far from the warmth of the Sun, Uranus moves slowly through the cold depths of space. It has a ring system and a collection of small moons, but there's something that makes it a bit different from the other planets — its axis is tilted, so it orbits the Sun on its side. One possible reason for this is that long ago, the planet was smashed into by another world.

Uranus's atmosphere is mostly composed of hydrogen, helium, and methane. No one knows for certain what lies under its thick blanket of clouds, but it could be a core of ice and rock.

he bright splotches
ou can see here
re auroras.

Neptune

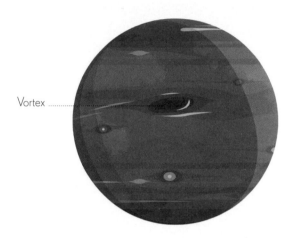

Vortex ....

Dark vortexes and bright clouds
sometimes appear in Neptune's
deep blue atmosphere.

It's difficult to imagine just how far away from the Sun the planet
Neptune is. It's around 4.5 billion km (2.8 billion miles) away,
which means that if you could drive at 80 km (50 miles) per hour
through space, it would take you more than 6,000 years to reach it.

At this enormous distance, it takes Neptune 164 Earth years to go
all the way around the Sun once. Fierce winds whip through the
planet's thick atmosphere, which is made up of hydrogen and helium,
along with other gases like methane. The tremendous temperatures
and pressures inside Neptune make some scientists think that
diamonds could be forming and swirling through the planet's
hidden depths. Imagine rain made of diamonds!

The Voyager
space probe visite
Neptune in 198

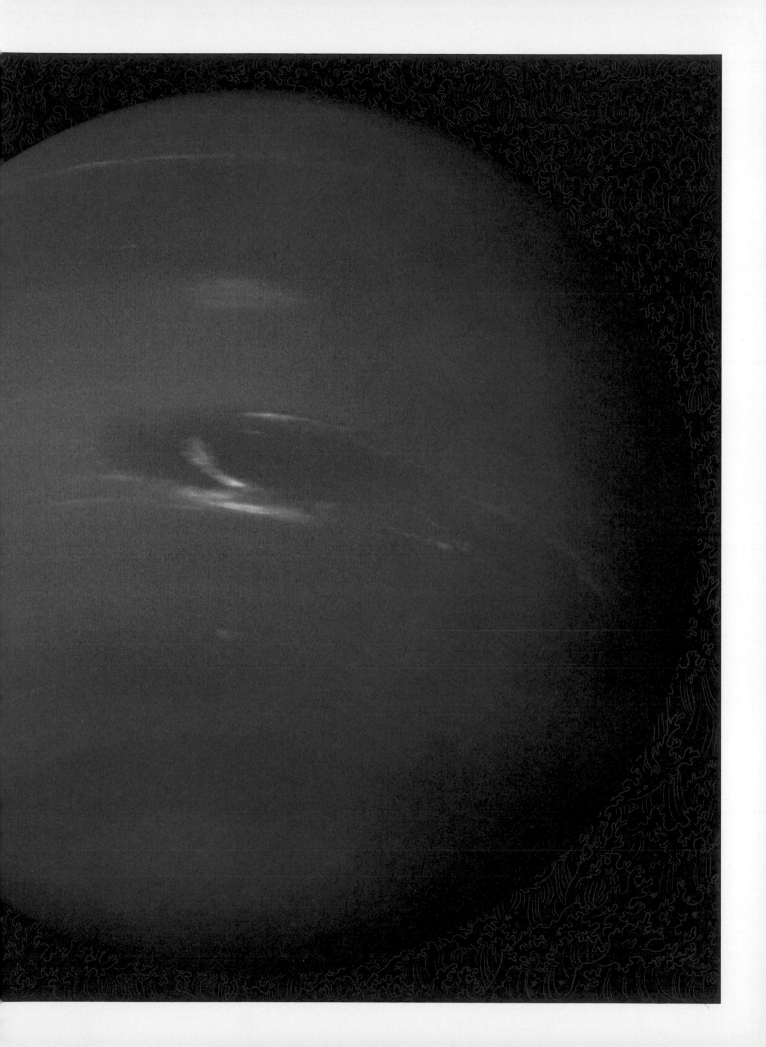

Triton's southern
hemisphere

Triton

Where did Neptune's largest moon, Triton, come from? That might seem like a strange question, but it's one that astronomers have been thinking about for a long time. That's because some scientists believe that Triton may have once floated freely through the outer Solar System, before being captured by Neptune's gravity.

Like many of the objects in the distant reaches of our planetary neighbourhood, Triton is a cold, icy world. Look closely and you'll see dark smudges in places — it's thought these are streaks left by powerful geysers shooting up plumes of nitrogen from under this moon's frozen surface.

Triton is named after the Greek god
of the sea, who was thought to calm
stormy waters using his conch shell.

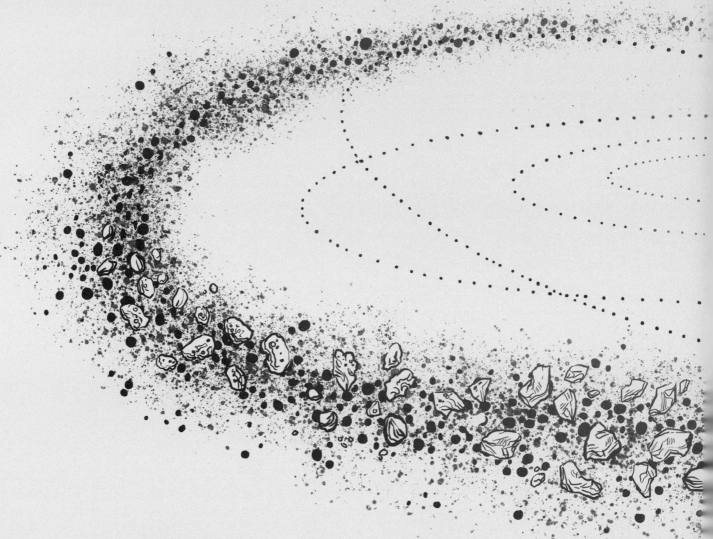

The Kuiper Belt

The first Kuiper Belt
Object, after Pluto, was
discovered in 1992.

The Kuiper Belt lies beyond the orbit of Neptune.

If you travel beyond Neptune you'll eventually reach a gigantic doughnut-shaped region called the Kuiper Belt. It contains thousands of small frozen objects left over from the Solar System's early history, and is home to Pluto and three other dwarf planets, Haumea, Eris, and Makemake. Scientists are still piecing together the story of this faraway region. It seems that some of its objects were flung here long ago by the gravity of Neptune and the other gas giants.

The Kuiper Belt is so far from Earth that astronomers use powerful telescopes to study it. Recently, though, a mission called New Horizons explored this region. After many years of travelling, the probe was able to fly past some of the Kuiper Belt's icy treasures.

Pluto

In 1930, American astronomer Clyde Tombaugh was searching through photographs of the night sky, looking for objects hiding in the outer Solar System. In one set of pictures he discovered a dot of light moving against the stars. That tiny speck was the world in the Kuiper Belt we now call Pluto.

For a long time everyone thought of Pluto as the ninth planet — the smallest of them all. But new discoveries revealed there were other, similar, icy worlds living in this distant part of our Solar System. As our understanding changed, Pluto was put in a new category — we now call it a dwarf planet.

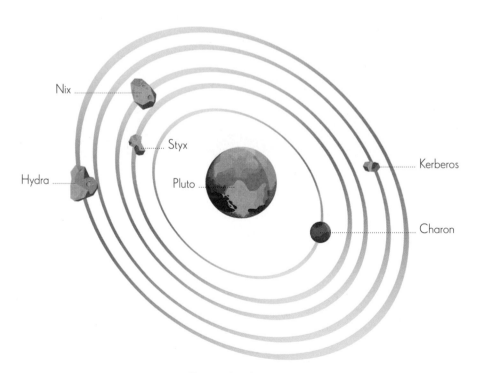

Nix

Styx

Pluto

Hydra

Kerberos

Charon

Pluto and its five moons

Charon

Pluto has a family of
five moons - the largest
is called Charon.

Pluto

Can you see the
shape of a heart
on Pluto's surface?

Frozen
fields

Pluto has a thin atmosphere
made up of nitrogen,
methane, and other gases.

At first glance, you might not think there's anything remarkable about this picture, but it is truly extraordinary. It's not a model from a movie set or a computer-generated image dreamed up by an artist. It's a real picture of the surface of Pluto, captured by a camera on the New Horizons spacecraft.

In this panorama, hills rise up from sweeping plains, while towering mountains and jagged terrain casts shadows in the faint light of the distant Sun. But those mountains aren't composed of rock and soil, like the peaks you and I know on Earth. Instead, they're made of water ice, and the landscape around them is frozen nitrogen.

The mountains and plains of Pluto can be seen here in extraordinary detail.

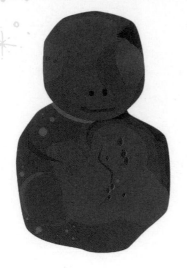

Arrokoth probably got its shape when two icy objects slowly collided and squished together.

An ancient snowman

This peculiar looking object is known as Arrokoth. It lives in the outer Solar System, inside the Kuiper Belt. Though it might not look it, it's actually one of the most exciting and important celestial objects that humans have ever visited with a space probe. What makes it so interesting is its great age — it's roughly 4.5 billion years old — and how well preserved it is after billions of years floating in the depths of space. It has survived untouched for all that time, so scientists hope studying it will tell us about how our planetary family formed.

Arrokoth was firs
spotted in 201
by the Hubbl
Space Telescope

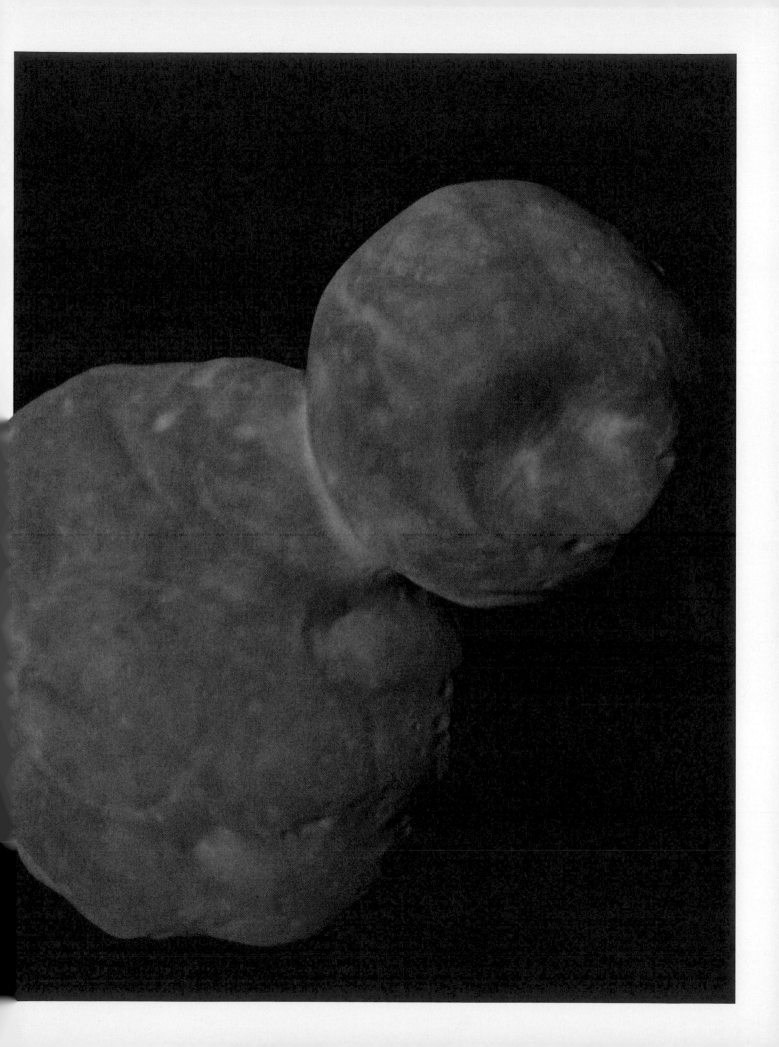

Comets

Some comets
develop two tails -
one made of gas
and one made of dust.

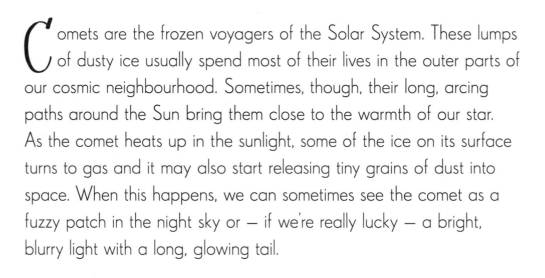

Comets are the frozen voyagers of the Solar System. These lumps
of dusty ice usually spend most of their lives in the outer parts of
our cosmic neighbourhood. Sometimes, though, their long, arcing
paths around the Sun bring them close to the warmth of our star.
As the comet heats up in the sunlight, some of the ice on its surface
turns to gas and it may also start releasing tiny grains of dust into
space. When this happens, we can sometimes see the comet as a
fuzzy patch in the night sky or — if we're really lucky — a bright,
blurry light with a long, glowing tail.

This picture of Come
Hale—Bopp was take
in 1997. The blu
streak is the gas ta

Cliffs on a comet

Comet 67P

On Comet 67P, also known as Churyumov–Gerasimenko, huge, icy cliffs rise over a frozen landscape covered in boulders. The land is cracked and rugged, and scientists describe the texture of some areas as "goosebumps" and "dinosaur eggs". There are giant pits where jets of gas and dust burst out into the bright sunlight.

We know all this because a European spacecraft called Rosetta travelled to 67P and captured spectacular close-up pictures of its surface. While it circled the comet, Rosetta made important scientific discoveries. From the data it gathered, scientists are hoping to learn more about how comets could have helped make planets like Earth.

Some of the cliffs on Comet 67P
are several hundred metres high.

Cliffs of ice and
dust, as seen by the
Rosetta spacecraft

Scientists use computer
models to work out
the size and shape
of the Oort Cloud.

Some scientists think there could
be well over a trillion objects
in the Oort Cloud.

The Oort Cloud

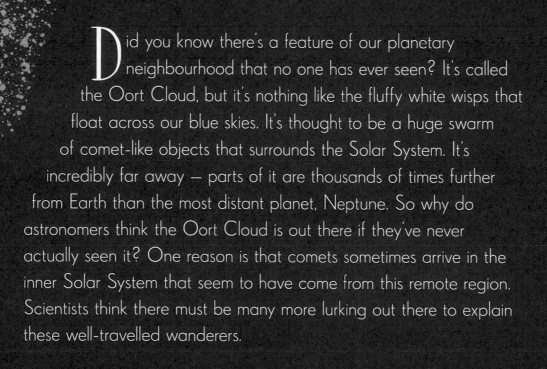

D id you know there's a feature of our planetary
neighbourhood that no one has ever seen? It's called
the Oort Cloud, but it's nothing like the fluffy white wisps that
float across our blue skies. It's thought to be a huge swarm
of comet-like objects that surrounds the Solar System. It's
incredibly far away — parts of it are thousands of times further
from Earth than the most distant planet, Neptune. So why do
astronomers think the Oort Cloud is out there if they've never
actually seen it? One reason is that comets sometimes arrive in the
inner Solar System that seem to have come from this remote region.
Scientists think there must be many more lurking out there to explain
these well-travelled wanderers.

'Oumuamua tumbles through space, spinning roughly once every seven hours.

Interstellar visitors

In the last few years, astronomers have come face to face with the first-known visitors from distant star systems beyond the Sun's realm. These two alien travellers weren't the kind you might imagine from sci-fi movies, though. Instead, they were an asteroid and a comet that must have been flung from their faraway home system long ago.

The asteroid, called 'Oumuamua (oh-MOO-ah-MOO-ah), was seen zipping through our Solar System in 2017, while the comet, Borisov, was spotted in 2019. Astronomers raced to study the two interstellar objects before they zoomed away forever, in the hope of learning more about the mysterious places from which they came.

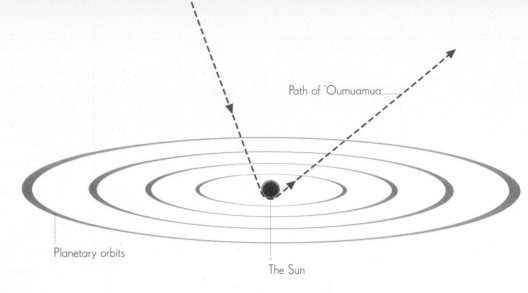

Path of 'Oumuamua ....

Planetary orbits

The Sun

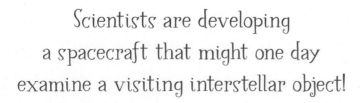

Scientists are developing
a spacecraft that might one day
examine a visiting interstellar object!

Scientists think the Milky Way
contains around 200-400 billion stars.

The Milky Way

Our Sun is one of billions of stars that swirl through space in
an enormous gathering known as a galaxy. We call this home
galaxy of ours the Milky Way. That's because from our perspective
— sitting among this huge swarm of stars — the rest of the galaxy
looks like a milky, misty ribbon of light.

If you could fly away from the Milky Way and look back, you would
see that the galaxy is shaped like a disc with a ball-shaped centre.
Within this disc there are whirl-like structures called spiral arms —
we live inside one of these.

NASA telescopes
use infrared and
X-ray light to
reveal the beauty
of the Milky Way.

Stars

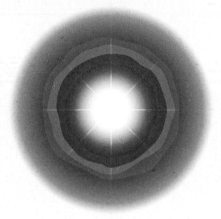

Every night, the sky glitters with the light of countless twinkling stars. They appear as tiny points to us only because they are so far away. If we could travel to explore them up close we'd see that they are, like our Sun, blazing balls that shine as matter fuses, or joins together, inside them.

Since the stars are so distant, it takes a long time for their light to reach us. For example, the light we see now from the middle star in Orion's Belt, Alnilam, started its journey almost 2,000 years ago. When you look at the sparkling night sky, you're actually gazing deep into the past. Isn't that amazing?

Stars can have life-spans of billions of years!

This group of stars was photographed by the Hubble Space Telescope.

In 2016, astronomers discovered a planet orbiting Proxima Centauri.

Proxima Centauri

W here the pale band of the Milky Way runs through the southern hemisphere constellation of Centaurus, the night sky is brimming with stars. Nestled among these gems is a faint red star called Proxima Centauri.

Though you'd need a good telescope to see it, this little fleck of light is quite special — at around four light-years away, Proxima Centauri is the nearest star to the Sun. It is still a huge distance from us, though — if the Sun was the size of a pen nib, then Proxima Centauri would be nearly 29 km (18 miles) away!

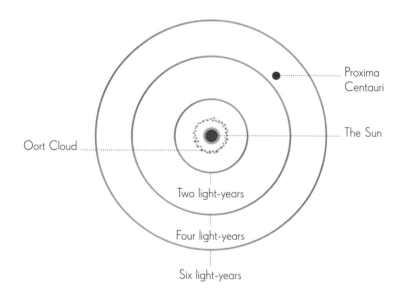

Oort Cloud

Proxima Centauri

The Sun

Two light-years

Four light-years

Six light-years

This image of Proxima Centauri was captured by the Hubble Space Telescope.

Enormous jets of material sometimes shoot
out from protostars, like beams from a lighthouse.

The youngest stars

Stars are born within enormous clouds of gas and dust floating in space. Astronomers think the process begins when clumps start to form deep inside the cold, dark haze. Over time, the clumps grow as they gather material from around them — a bit like how a snowball gets bigger. Eventually, a spinning object known as a protostar forms. If it grows large enough, nuclear reactions can fire up within a protostar's centre and it becomes a fully fledged, shining sun.

Scientists still have lots of questions about exactly how all this happens. This is partly because baby stars are often hidden by the dusty gas clouds in which they are born — to investigate, astronomers need special telescopes and cameras to peer through the murk.

This protostar is
gathering material from
the gas surrounding it.

The Trapezium Cluster

What do you think is causing these swirling gas clouds to glow such a beautiful ruby-red colour? Look at the very centre of the view, where the clouds are brightest, and you'll see the culprits: a group of four sparkling newborn stars. This little collection is known as the Trapezium Cluster, and it lies nestled in the heart of the Orion Nebula.

The stars in the Trapezium are scorching hot and they blaze brightly. Their light energizes the gas around them, causing it to give off a pinkish-red glow. Curiosities like the Trapezium Cluster are fascinating to astronomers because by studying them we can learn more about the early lives of stars and the groups they form.

You can spot the Trapezium Cluster
from Earth using a small telescope.

The Trapezium Cluster

Can you see the
cluster in the centre
of the nebula?

The heart of the Orion Nebula

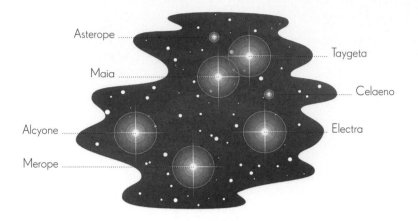

Asterope

Maia

Alcyone

Merope

Taygeta

Celaeno

Electra

Star clusters

When you gaze up the night sky, you'll see little groups of stars huddled together. Astronomers call these groups star clusters. Some of the easiest to see are open star clusters — collections of bright young stars that have formed together in space.

The Pleiades is a famous open star cluster that sits in the constellation of Taurus, the Bull. There are more than 1,200 infant stars in this dazzling crowd. Recent measurements suggest that the stars in the Pleiades are only around 130 million years old!

Our Sun probably formed within a cluster of stars that has now spread out across the Milky Way.

The Pleiades is also known as the Seven Sisters.

Birth of a planet

How exactly do planets form? That is a question that has had scientists scratching their heads for centuries. To look for clues to this mystery, astronomers today use powerful telescopes to study newly formed stars, far beyond our own Solar System. They do this because many of these distant young stars are surrounded by enormous, circular clouds of dust and gas, called protoplanetary discs. Astronomers think that swirling inside these discs are the raw ingredients from which worlds can be made, so by examining them we can learn more about how a planet is constructed. Scientists have already uncovered signs of planetary building blocks, such as small pebbles, around some young stars.

This illustration shows a protoplanetary disc surrounding a young star.

Billions of years ago, our Sun
was probably surrounded by a
protoplanetary disc.

Exoplanets

So far, more than 4,000 exoplanets have been found orbiting around distant stars.

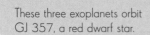

These three exoplanets orbit GJ 357, a red dwarf star.

GJ357d

GJ357b

GJ357c

While we don't know if there are other life forms elsewhere in the Milky Way, we do know there are other planets out there. Thousands of them, in fact! These worlds are known as exoplanets.

There is still a lot about exoplanets that we don't know. Many of them seem to be very strange places indeed. Some could have bubbling surfaces of molten rock, while others have ferocious winds that race around their atmosphere. Some are giant worlds made of gas that orbit close to their fiery parent star — we don't have anything like that in our Solar System. In the coming decades, new telescopes should allow us to take a closer look at some of these faraway planets. Perhaps we'll even find one just like Earth!

Vega

The light we see today from Vega left the star's surface around 25 years ago.

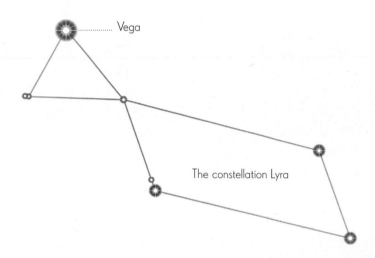

Vega

The constellation Lyra

Vega is one of the brightest stars in the night sky. It lies in the constellation Lyra, close to the rich star fields of the Milky Way. If you cast your eyes towards this brilliant star on a clear autumn night in the northern hemisphere, you'll see it has a white hue, with a slight hint of blue. Gaze around and you'll soon see stars of other colours too — some orange, some yellow, others zingy blue.

Why are stars different colours? It all depends on their temperature. The hotter a star is, the bluer and whiter its light — cooler stars are more yellow and orange. Some of the coolest stars in the galaxy have a deep red-orange glow, like embers in a fireplace.

Vega was the first star — after our own Sun — to be photographed, in 1850.

Betelgeuse is about
720 light-years
away from Earth.

You could squeeze around 900 trillion
Earths inside Betelgeuse!

Betelgeuse

One of the most mysterious stars in the constellation Orion is the red-hued Betelgeuse. It is in the very final stages of its life. After consuming much of its fuel, it has bloated to become a vast, red supergiant measuring more than 1.2 billion km (746 million miles) across. If the Sun was the size of a pea, Betelgeuse would be over 7 metres (23 feet) wide! When it dies, Betelgeuse will likely explode as a brilliant supernova. Astronomers aren't sure exactly when this will happen, but some estimates suggest it could detonate in the next 100,000 years.

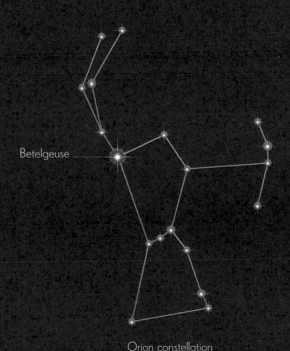

Betelgeuse ············

Orion constellation

Eta Carinae

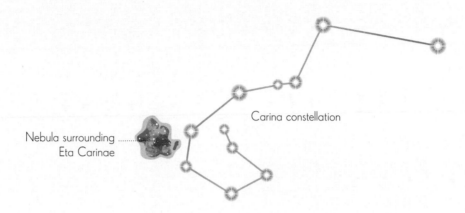

Nebula surrounding
Eta Carinae

Carina constellation

Y ou wouldn't know it if you looked at the softly shimmering star fields in the constellation Carina, but this stretch of the southern hemisphere night skies is full of violent activity. Within Carina there is an incredible stellar system called Eta Carinae, which is composed of two stars. The reason it is so fascinating is that one of the pair has recently experienced unimaginably huge eruptions. Scientists think it is probably close to the end of its life.

Eta Carinae is surrounded by a peanut-shaped cloud of material and glowing wisps of gas — these were probably created during previous explosions of the dying star. Eventually, Eta Carinae will detonate in one final, massive, explosion, called a supernova. As it does, it will shoot material out into space that may one day form the beginnings of a new generation of stars.

Eta Carinae is so far away that the events we see today actually happened over 8,400 years ago.

ta Carinae
xploded several
mes in the
9th century.

The most famous supernova of recent times, SN1987A, occurred within a nearby galaxy in 1987.

Supernova

Sometimes a star can explode in a violent blast that astronomers call a supernova. These spectacular events can occur in different ways. One type of supernova happens when a massive star gets old and runs out of the fuel that keeps it shining. When this happens, its centre implodes, producing an explosion that destroys the star.

Another kind of supernova occurs when the core of a long-dead star, known as a white dwarf, rips chunks of the atmosphere from a nearby star. If the white dwarf pulls enough material onto itself, it can explode, creating an enormous stellar firework that can be seen across huge cosmic distances.

Supernova

The colours in th
picture highlight th
shockwave and du
ring in the afterma
of SN1987A

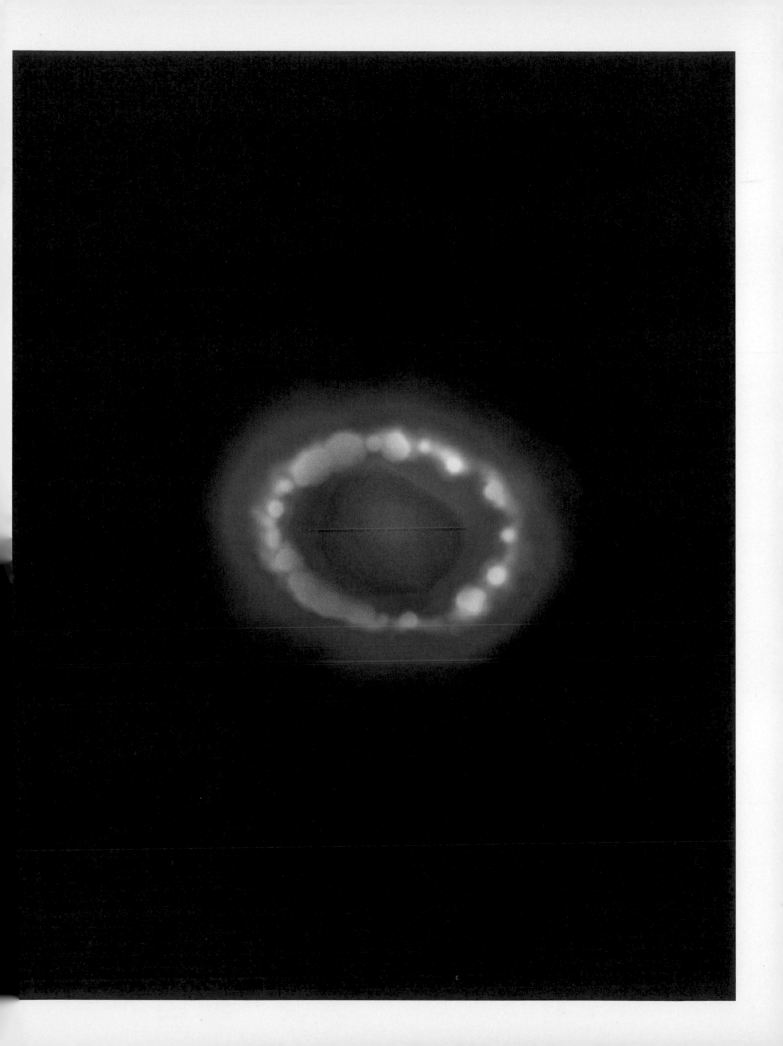

Neutron stars are typically
only around 20 kilometres
(12 miles) in diameter.

Neutron star

N eutron stars are the zombies of interstellar space. These amazing objects are created in the fiery explosion that occurs at the end of a massive star's life. Neutron stars are made up of a super-dense material consisting of tiny subatomic particles called neutrons. A sandgrain-sized fleck of neutron star matter would weigh roughly 500 million kg (550,000 tons) — about the same as 1,500 jumbo jets put together.

Some neutron stars blast beams of radio waves out across space. If the beams pass over Earth, as the neutron star spins, we can detect a throbbing radio signal. Astronomers call these objects "pulsars".

Neutron star ....

.... Magnetic field lines

Can you see the two
bright spots in the
centre? The neutron star
the one on the right.

Black hole

Black holes are among the most mysterious objects in the Universe. It's impossible to see them directly, and even the world's cleverest scientists do not understand exactly how they work. What we do know is that black holes are an example of nature behaving very strangely indeed.

These curious spherical regions warp the space around them dramatically — they have such a strong gravitational pull that even the fastest thing we know of, light itself, is dragged into them. This means they're almost totally black. Some black holes are thought to be born in the explosion that happens when a very massive star dies. There are even bulkier black holes hiding in the hearts of many galaxies too — even our own Milky Way has one!

The galaxy M87 has an enormous black hole at its centre, with a mass 6.5 billion times the mass of the Sun.

This image is our best-ever view of a black hole's surroundings.

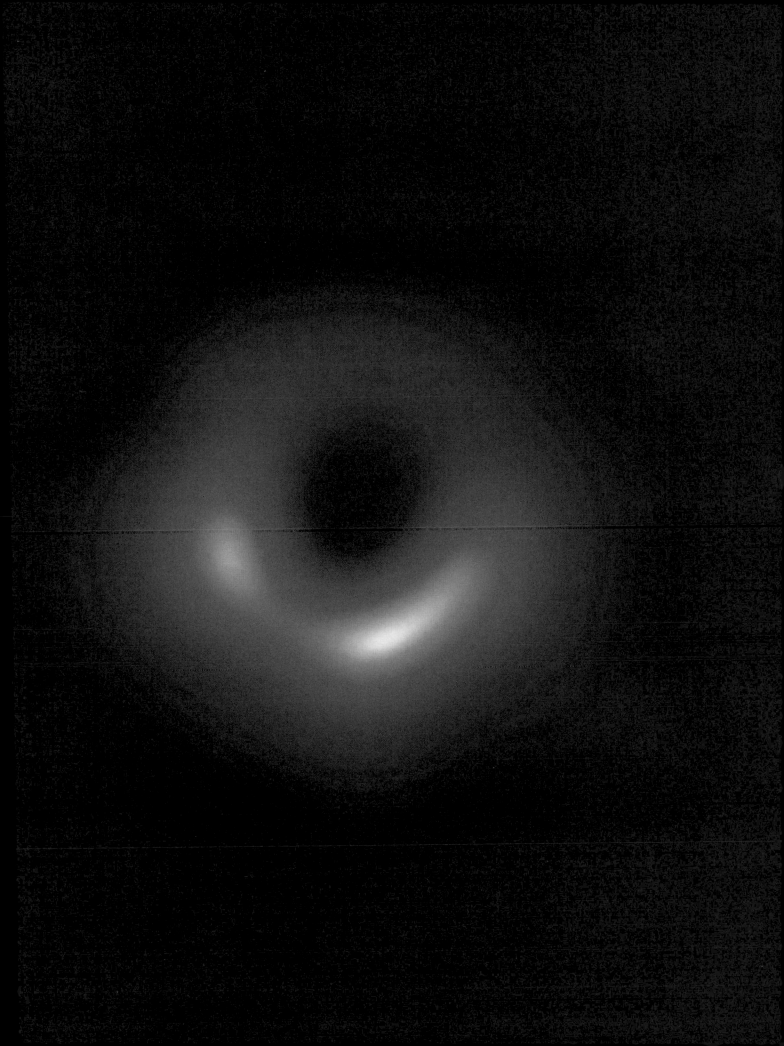

Globular cluster

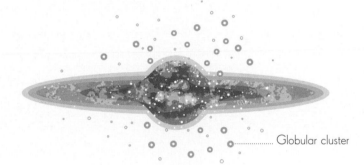

.... Globular cluster

Side view of the Milky Way

Where do you think you can see the most breath-taking view of the stars? Looking up at a cloudless desert sky perhaps, or far out at sea on the very blackest of nights? The answer, in fact, is not on Earth at all — it's the view from inside a globular cluster.

These extraordinary objects contain thousands upon thousands of dazzling stars, all packed tightly together in the shape of a ball. Some of the Milky Way's globular clusters could be the leftovers from smaller galaxies that were gobbled up by our galaxy a long time ago. If there are any planets orbiting the stars within these globular clusters, their night skies will surely be awe-inspiring, with countless brilliant points of light filling almost every patch of darkness.

The globular cluster Omega Centauri
contains at least 1.7 million stars!

Omega Centauri is the largest globular cluster in the Milky Way.

Nebula

If you were to zoom across the Milky Way in a spaceship, you wouldn't just encounter stars and planets along the way. You'd also pass gigantic clouds of dust and gas that are scattered all throughout the galaxy. Astronomers have a name for a cosmic cloud like this: it's called a nebula, and there are several different kinds.

Some, for example, are places where stars are being born, and where gas mingles with blazing new suns to create spectacular glowing shapes. Others are the ghosts of long-dead stars — shining ripples of gas that mark where a star once exploded. With powerful telescopes, astronomers can even study these stunning forms in distant galaxies, far beyond our own.

The Carina Nebula in the southern hemisphere is so bright you can see it without a telescope!

Clockwise from top left; the Witch Head Nebula; the Pipe Nebula; the Lagoon Nebula; the Crab supernova remnant; and the Necklace Nebula

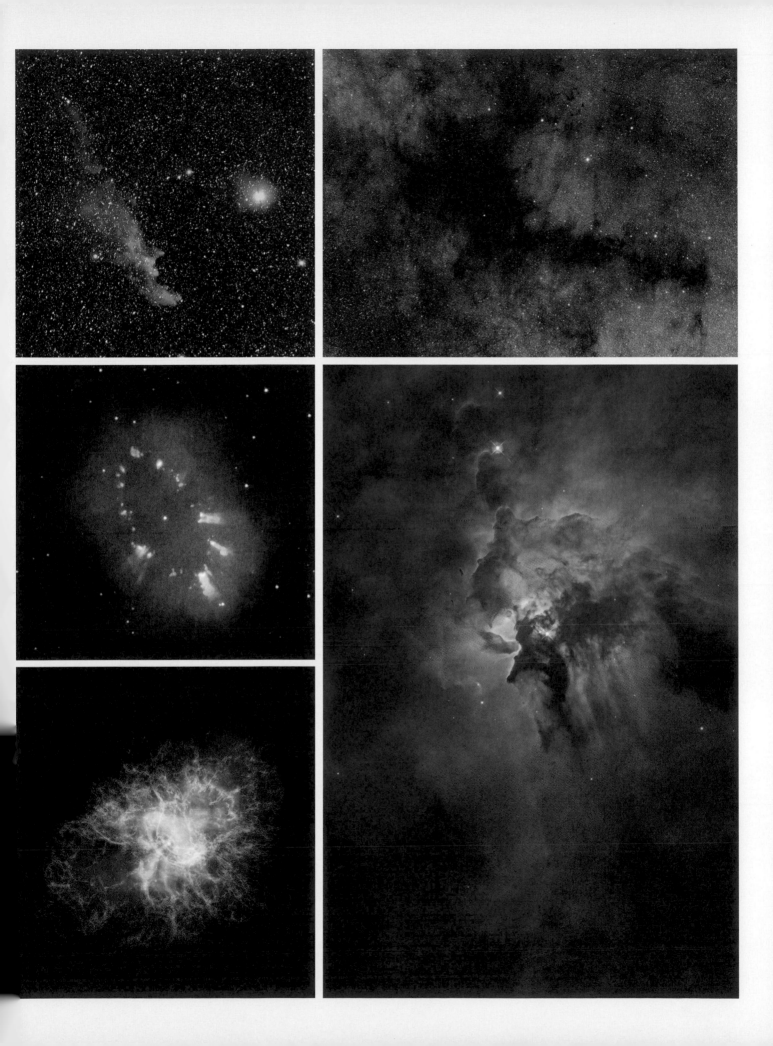

The striking reddish-pink colour of an emission nebula comes mainly from glowing hydrogen gas.

Emission nebula

Have you noticed that a lot of pictures of the night sky and distant galaxies show splashes of bright pink and red? Each one is a glimmering gas cloud that astronomers call an emission nebula. Some stargazers refer to them as stellar nurseries, because they are regions where new stars are forming inside vast swirls of gas and dust.

An emission nebula gives off its colourful glow because the gases inside are energized by light from hot, young stars that have been born within the cloud. Pick up a good pair of binoculars, and on certain nights you can probably see an emission nebula for yourself!

The Lagoon Nebula sits within the constellation Sagittarius.

Planetary nebula

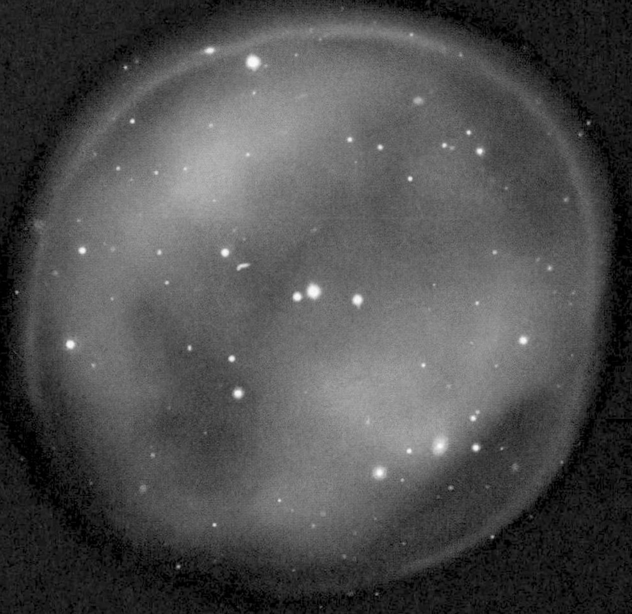

The Southern Owl Nebula

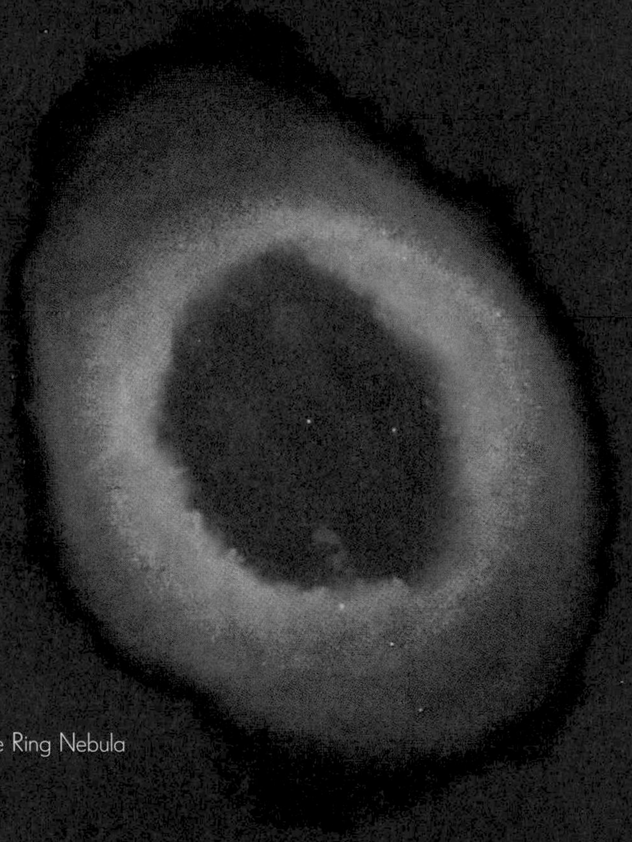

The Ring Nebula

The Ring Nebula is around
10 trillion km (6.2 trillion miles) across.

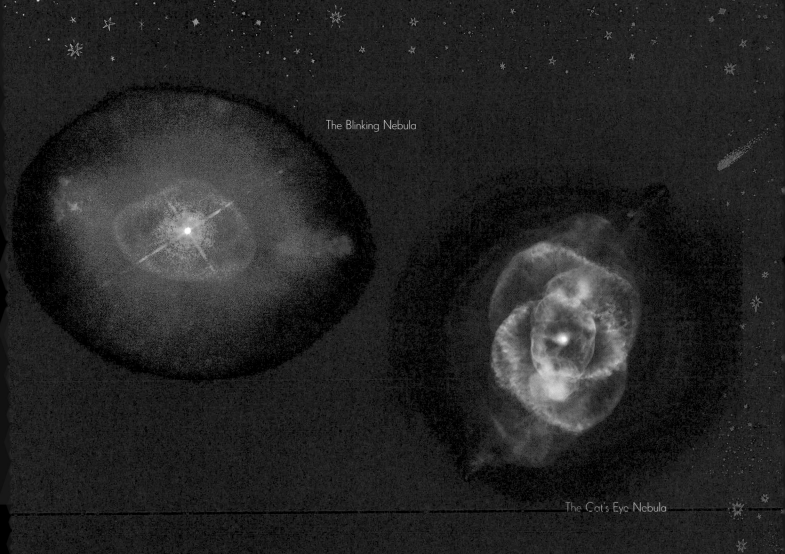

The Blinking Nebula

The Cat's Eye Nebula

Imagine you were out on a clear night peering at the stars through a telescope eyepiece and you stumbled across a sight like this — what would you say it looked like? To some of the astronomers who first saw these distant celestial objects, the rounded, glowing gas clouds resembled faraway planets, so they became known as planetary nebulae.

In fact, they're nothing to do with planets at all. A planetary nebula is what bursts into being at the end of some stars' lives. Each nebula you see here was produced when a star, probably quite similar to our Sun, grew old and shed its atmosphere. As the star's bulk puffed out into space its searing core was revealed. This core still glows today and it pumps energy into the star's jettisoned atmosphere, making it shine in all kinds of fantastic colours.

Dark nebula

Dark nebula ......

The temperature of the
dust swirling inside
the Horsehead Nebula
is about -250 °C (-418 °F).

This nebula is called
the Horsehead
Nebula — it's easy
to see why!

Not all the clouds of dust and gas in our galaxy glow brightly.
Many simply lurk in the darkness of space, appearing only
as silhouettes against brighter backgrounds or dense fields of stars.
These cold, so-called "dark" nebulae can be found throughout outer
space, and they include some of the most recognizable astronomical
objects, such as the Horsehead Nebula in the constellation Orion
and the Coalsack Nebula in the constellation Crux.

By capturing light from these objects that our eyes can't pick up,
professional telescopes have shown that some dark nebulae have
what may be the beginnings of stars forming within them.

Reflection nebula

Peer deep into the mystical dust clouds in this faraway corner of our galaxy, and you will see something magical happening. The inner regions of this enormous nebula — known as Messier 78 — appear to be shining an otherworldly blue colour. There are no wizards at work here, though. In fact, what's happening is that the billowing dust swirls in Messier 78 are scattering the light from stars inside the nebula. The dust scatters the blue in the starlight more than it does the other colours, which gives the nebula its milky blue appearance.

The famous Pleiades star cluster
is surrounded by a faint reflection nebula.

Reflection nebula

This reflection nebula called Messier 78 It can be found in th constellation Orio

Galactic Centre

If you're walking in the countryside on a misty day, it's sometimes hard to see the beautiful landscape in the distance. Astronomers have a similar problem when they look towards the heart of the Milky Way, known as the Galactic Centre. Instead of mist, though, astronomers face huge, obscuring dust clouds floating within our galaxy.

To study the Galactic Centre, and to create spectacular pictures of it, astronomers use special telescopes and cameras that can see infrared radiation — a kind of light that is given off by celestial objects. Unlike ordinary light, it can travel through dusty wisps in space, allowing us to get a clear picture of the hidden galactic hub.

Galactic Centre

The heart of the Milky Way

The way stars are moving around the Galactic Centre suggests there's a hefty black hole lurking within.

This infrared image reveals hundreds of thousands of stars in the Galactic Centre.

The Pillars of Creation are found in the Eagle Nebula, about 5,870 light-years from Earth.

The Pillars of Creation

The Pillars of Creation

The billowing clouds of dust and gas where stars form don't last forever. They are gradually sculpted and eventually destroyed by particle-filled winds and the harsh light produced by the stars around them — often the very ones they gave birth to.

The spectacular Pillars of Creation, in the constellation Serpens, give us a glimpse of this extraordinary process in action. The name comes from their location within an enormous stellar nursery called the Eagle Nebula, and the fact that there is a smattering of baby stars cocooned inside them. These dense fingers of gas and dust will ultimately break up and drift out into the galaxy, their glowing forms and swirling shapes never to be seen again.

In this image, the green is nitrogen and hydrogen, the red is sulphur, and the blue is oxygen.

Every human body contains some elements - made by an exploding star - that once floated within a supernova remnant.

Supernova remnant

When a star dies in a violent supernova explosion, it doesn't simply leave behind a boring patch of empty space. The grand finale of these amazing firework displays is the formation of a glowing supernova remnant. These are clouds of rapidly expanding material that surge out into the void where the star once lived. As powerful shockwaves race outwards, they can also create ghostly tendrils of light that may shine for thousands of years after the dazzling supernova blast has faded.

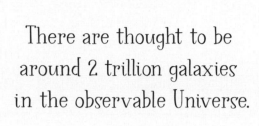

There are thought to be
around 2 trillion galaxies
in the observable Universe.

Galaxy

If our eyes were like enormous telescopes, we'd see that — beyond the stars of the Milky Way — the cosmos is full of countless smudges of light. These distant, fuzzy patches are actually enormous collections of stars that astronomers call galaxies.

Like humans, galaxies come in all different shapes and sizes. Our Milky Way, for example, is a spiral galaxy — it has twisting "arms" like a whirlpool. Elliptical galaxies are more rounded, without this beautiful structure, while others, known as irregular galaxies, are little more than a random jumble of stars. One reason astronomers are so interested in learning about faraway galaxies is that they may help us piece together the story of how the Milky Way formed. This is because looking deep into space reveals galaxies that lived a long time ago, and these could provide information about the ancestors of the Milky Way.

Clockwise from top;
a majestic spiral
galaxy; a giant
elliptical galaxy;
a dwarf irregular galaxy

The Local Group

The furthest member of the Local Group
to us is a galaxy called UGC 4879, about
4.4 million light-years away.

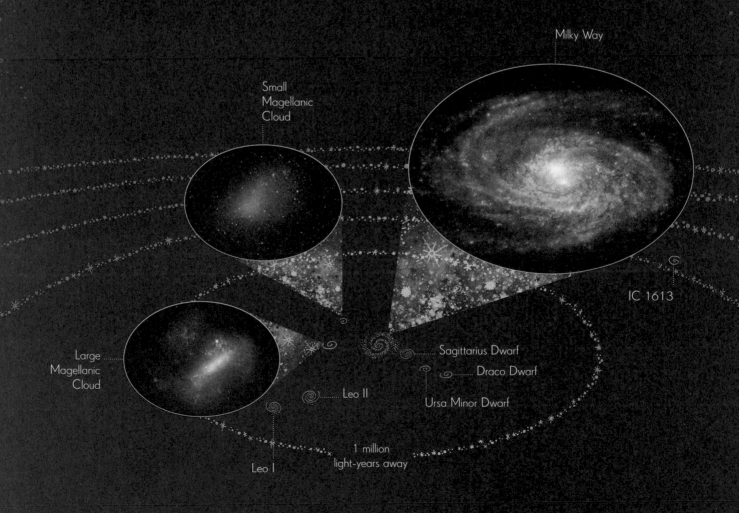

Milky Way

Small
Magellanic
Cloud

IC 1613

Large
Magellanic
Cloud

Sagittarius Dwarf

Draco Dwarf

Leo II

Ursa Minor Dwarf

Leo I

1 million
light-years away

2 millio
light-years

Y ou might know the neighbours next door, or have friends on your street, but did you know that the Milky Way has its own neighbours in space? They're a band of nearby galaxies known as the Local Group.

The larger members of the Local Group include the enormous Andromeda and Triangulum Galaxies and the Magellanic Clouds, which float close to the Milky Way. Astronomers think there are about 75 galaxies in the Local Group.

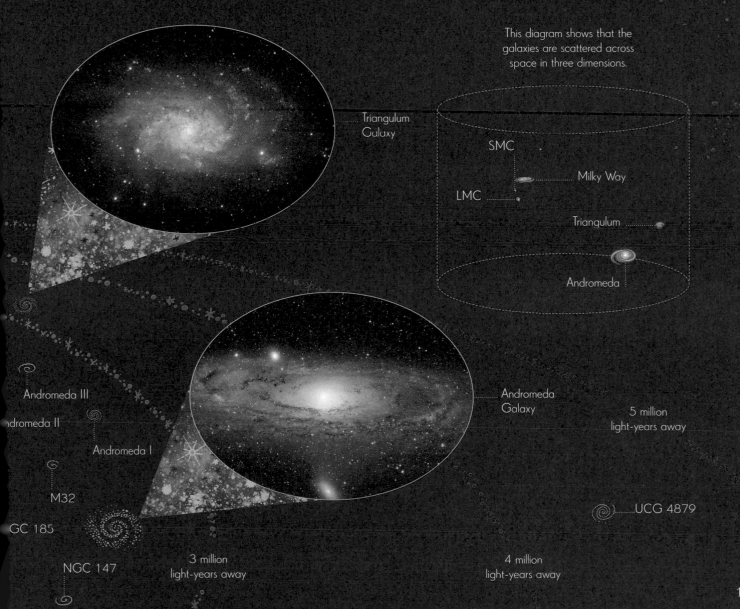

This diagram shows that the galaxies are scattered across space in three dimensions.

Triangulum Galaxy

SMC

Milky Way

LMC

Triangulum

Andromeda

Andromeda Galaxy

5 million light-years away

Andromeda III

ndromeda II

Andromeda I

M32

UCG 4879

GC 185

NGC 147

3 million light-years away

4 million light-years away

Dwarf galaxy

Some of the larger galaxies sprinkled across the cosmos are accompanied by smaller galactic friends. These so-called "dwarf" galaxies might not have the billions of stars of their larger and heftier buddies, but they nonetheless have fascinating stories to tell.

Some dwarf galaxies appear to be responsible for creating huge ribbons of stars that loop around larger galaxies. Scientists call these ribbons stellar streams, and by studying them they may be able to learn more about what happened in our galaxy's wild, violent past. For example, astronomers are examining the stream of stars one nearby dwarf galaxy, the Sagittarius Dwarf, seems to have strewn across space. They think they have figured out what's happening — the Sagittarius Dwarf is slowly merging with the Milky Way.

There are more than 25 dwarf galaxies zooming around our own Milky Way.

The Milky Way

Stream of stars

Dwarf galaxy

The Large Magellanic Cloud is home to many glowing gas clouds, including one that resembles a tarantula!

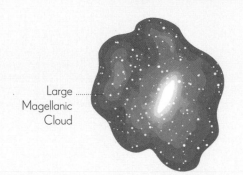

Large Magellanic Cloud

Small Magellanic Cloud

The Magellanic Clouds

In a swathe of the glittering night skies of the southern hemisphere, in the constellations of Dorado, Mensa, and nearby Tucana, are two misty patches of light. These glowing objects lie beyond the borders of our Milky Way, and they are known as the Large and Small Magellanic Clouds. They're not really clouds, though. In fact, they're two neighbouring galaxies — albeit small ones!

This cosmic pair has almost certainly been observed by the indigenous peoples of the southern hemisphere for thousands of years, though their English name comes from the European explorer Ferdinand Magellan, who spotted them while sailing the oceans in the 16th century.

This picture shows part of the Large Magellanic Cloud — it's full of dust, gas, and stars.

The Andromeda Galaxy is a spiral galaxy, like the Milky Way.

Spiral arm ....

The Andromeda Galaxy

The Andromeda Galaxy

Did you know that just using your eyes you can see more than 2 million light-years out into space? How can you possibly achieve this extraordinary feat? Well, all you need to do is look towards the constellation of Andromeda in the northern hemisphere on a clear autumn night. Among this collection of stars is a swirl of light known as the Andromeda Galaxy. This beautiful galaxy appears as a faint, glowing patch, shaped a bit like a grain of rice. The Andromeda Galaxy is roughly 2.6 million light-years from us, but it's getting closer. In fact, in around 6 billion years' time it will actually merge with the stars of our own Milky Way!

This galaxy is racing in our direction at more than 393,000 km (244,000 miles) per hour!

Starburst galaxy

Can you see the enormous red wisps flowing from the centre of this galaxy, known as Messier 82? Astronomers think they are swirls of gas and dust that have been swept into space by the winds from hefty stars living within the galaxy, as well as the effects of exploding stars. Galaxies that show signs of this activity are often called "starburst" galaxies, and the material shooting from them can be millions of degrees Celsius in places! Precisely how this amazing display unfolds is still a mystery, but the view — even from light-years away — is usually spectacular!

Messier 82 sits near the shoulder of the Great Bear - the constellation Ursa Major.

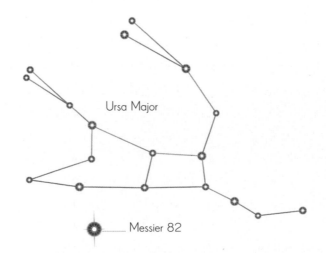

Ursa Major

Messier 82

The burst of re you can see here glowing hydrogen gc

Spiral galaxy

Among the most beautiful of all the kinds of galaxies are the spirals. These exquisite, sparkling whorls usually have a central region of older, yellower stars and several curving "arms", where stars are forming in droves, flecked with glowing red nebulae.

Astronomers are still trying to work out exactly how these spiral arms are made. Are they groups of stars moving around the centre of the galaxy like flocks of birds? Or are they the result of enormous ripples travelling through the galaxy's body? Perhaps by studying the spiral galaxy we live in – the Milky Way – we will find the answer!

The arms of spiral galaxies usually contain
lots of hot, young, blueish-white stars.

his spiral galaxy is
alled Messier 74.
is comparable in size
the Milky Way.

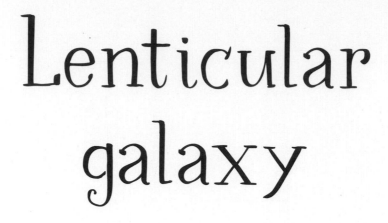

Lenticular galaxy

The light reaching us from the Spindle Galaxy left the galaxy 46 million years ago!

Some galaxies that drift through the depths of space aren't quite elliptical, and they don't look exactly like the galactic swirls we call spiral galaxies either. They're somewhere in between. Astronomers refer to these as "lenticular" galaxies, because they have a shape that's a bit like a simple lens — the kind you'd find in a basic magnifying glass.

This beautiful example is known as the Spindle Galaxy, or NGC 5866. It is side-on to Earth, so we can see its shape perfectly. Scientists are fascinated by lenticular galaxies like this one because they may be what some spiral galaxies become when they stop making stars.

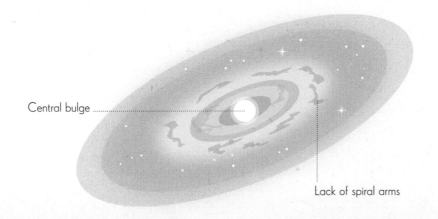

Central bulge ....

Lack of spiral arms

NCG 5866 is about 46 million light-years from Earth.

Elliptical galaxy

Jet of matter

There's a jet of matter, around a third of the size of our Milky Way, shooting from the black hole within the elliptical galaxy M87.

If you were a stargazer on a planet inside an elliptical galaxy, you'd probably get a bit bored with your night sky views. Though these rounded galaxies are often composed of billions of stars, they don't have the magnificent spiral shape of galaxies like the Milky Way. For the most part they also lack the glowing, star-forming gas clouds and dark, dusty nebulae seen in other kinds of galaxy. That doesn't make them any less interesting, though! Some of the largest elliptical galaxies seem to have grown huge by gobbling up other, smaller galaxies. Many of these vast balls of stars have supermassive black holes in their hearts. Who knows what lies inside?

These interacting galaxies are nicknamed "The Mice" because of their long tails!

Red gas appears as new stars form.

Interacting galaxies

With so many galaxies swarming around the cosmos, it's almost inevitable that sometimes they collide and merge, or at least get really close to one another. When this happens, the galaxies begin an extraordinary slow-motion dance as they start to feel the effects of each other's gravity. This process can last many hundreds of millions of years, and we can see examples of these so-called "interacting" galaxies all across space. As the galaxies spiral close to their partners, their shapes often become distorted — in some cases, they even fling off enormous, sparkling strands of stars as they pirouette together.

Some galaxy collisions show huge clumps of glowing, red gas where stars are forming in the unfolding chaos.

The most distant galaxies
in the Quintet are
roughly 277 million
light-years from Earth.

Stephan's Quintet

S ometimes, when we see faraway galaxies huddled together,
they're not really that close in space — it's just an illusion created
by the angle at which we're viewing them. Like distant mountain
peaks on the horizon, they look as if they're bunched up and all the
same distance away, but in fact they're spread far apart. That's
the case for this galactic gathering, known as Stephan's Quintet.
Four of the five galaxies really are twirling together through space in
a little swarm. Some have even bumped into each other in the past,
causing twisting arcs of stars to spray away from their glowing forms.
But the fifth galaxy isn't actually part of the group at all — it's much
closer to the Milky Way. Can you guess which is the odd one out?
That's right, it's the blue swirl in the top-left corner.

Stephan's Quintet was discovered by a
French astronomer called Édouard Stephan in 1876.

The Local Supercluster

The heart of the Local Supercluster is about
52 million light-years away from Earth.

I f you think about the Local Group of nearby galaxies as
neighbours on our street, the Local Supercluster is the sprawling
city that we all live in. This incredible swarm of galaxies, of many
different kinds, is thought to be home to thousands of inhabitants —
our Milky Way, in the suburbs of this galactic metropolis, is among
them. It is sometimes called the Virgo Supercluster because a large
part of it sits in the constellation we call Virgo. If you were to hold
your outstretched hand up to this patch of the night sky, you'd
be covering the locations of tens, if not hundreds, of galaxies in
the supercluster!

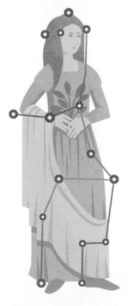

The Virgo constellation

This picture shows
Markarian's Chain
a swirl of galaxies that
lies in the centre of the
Local Supercluster

Gravitational lens

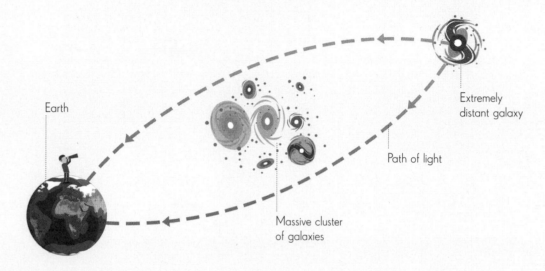

Earth

Extremely distant galaxy

Path of light

Massive cluster of galaxies

The humongous cluster of galaxies you can see here is so hefty that it is actually distorting space! The path of light travelling towards us from galaxies behind the cluster has been bent by its immense gravity — it is like what happens to light when it passes through an old window pane, or a telescope lens. This means that our view of distant galaxies is magnified and smeared, making them look like thin arcs of light.

The galaxy cluster in this gravitational lens weighs around 380 trillion times the mass of the Sun!

an you see the thin
s of light made by
s gravitational lens?

Gazing into the past

Almost every spot of light you can see in this picture is a faraway galaxy. This incredible panorama, known as the eXtreme Deep Field, was captured by the Hubble Space Telescope, a telescope that orbits Earth. It is one of humanity's furthest glimpses into the distant cosmos, and to produce it, Hubble gathered light for more than three weeks. In fact, when you look at this image you're staring roughly 13 billion years into the past — because that's how long light has been travelling towards Hubble's cameras from some of the faintest reddish-orange galaxies in the frame. Future space telescopes will try to see further than Hubble's masterpiece, in the hope of learning more about how our cosmos was constructed.

The Hubble Space Telescope has been taking pictures from orbit since 1990!

The eXtreme Deep Field shows us galaxies from billions of years ago.

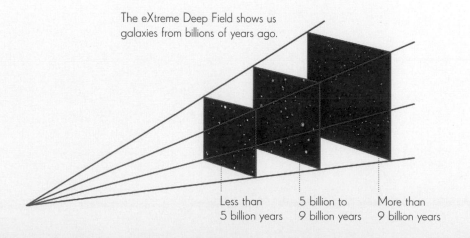

Less than 5 billion years

5 billion to 9 billion years

More than 9 billion years

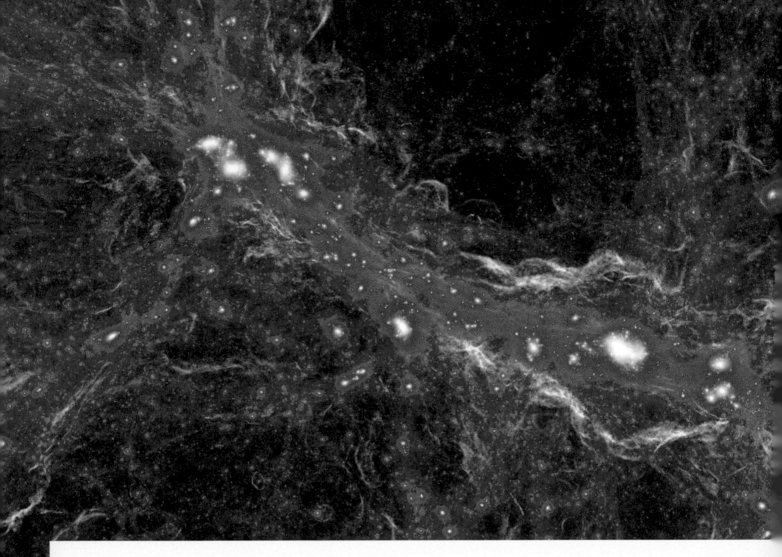

The cosmic web

This illustration shows clusters of galaxies linked together by gas filaments

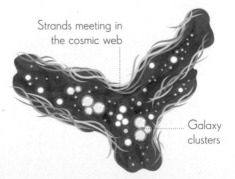

Strands meeting in the cosmic web

Galaxy clusters

By carefully charting the distances of numerous faraway galaxies, astronomers have been able to map the shape and structure of enormous sections of the Universe. They have found that the cosmos seems to have a texture similar to the inside of a sponge, with huge voids of relatively empty space surrounded by filaments, or threads, made of countless galaxies and other matter.

Scientists today use powerful supercomputers to examine how these strange shapes could have come about — we may be getting close to finding out the secrets of the cosmic web!

Huge clusters of galaxies may form
where strands of the cosmic web meet.

The cosmic glow

After exploring so much of space — visiting distant worlds and far-off galaxies — we now come to something that appears all over the cosmos. You and I can't see it, but special telescopes used by professional astronomers can. What is it? Well, it's a kind of light. Technically, this light is microwave radiation. It appears in every direction astronomers point their instruments, and is known as the Cosmic Microwave Background (CMB).

Astronomers think the Cosmic Microwave Background is the glow left over from the time just after the birth of the Universe — the blazing maelstrom that we know very little about, the Big Bang.

By studying the Cosmic Microwave Background, astronomers estimate that the Universe is around 13.75 billion years old.

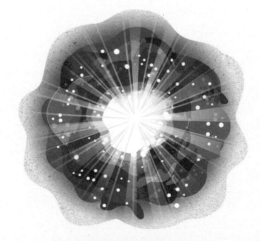

The Big Bang

The Local Group

The Milky Way

The Solar System

The journey

Even if you could travel at the speed of light,
it would still take you several million years
to leave the Local Group of galaxies!

The Local
Supercluster

The cosmic web

W hat an incredible adventure we've been on. We began by
staring up at the night sky, marvelling at sights that humans
have admired for millennia. As we travelled through the Solar System,
we saw that even close to home there are untold mysteries that
science has yet to explore. Leaving our planetary neighbourhood,
we ventured out into the Milky Way and the wonders scattered
within this enormous swirl of stars. Last of all, we explored the secrets
of the immense, distant realms of the Universe, littered with billions of
galaxies of every kind. But that's not really the end. Where will our
future exploration take us on this thrilling cosmic journey?

Northern constellations

The northern night sky rotates around a point close to the star Polaris in the constellation Ursa Minor.

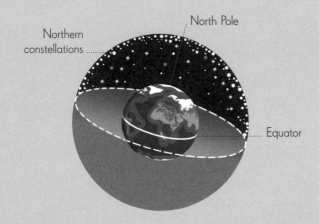

Northern constellations

North Pole

Equator

The night skies of the northern hemisphere are home to an incredible variety of glittering star fields that change with the seasons. In winter, the constellations Gemini, Taurus, and Auriga are sprinkled with beautiful star clusters that you can marvel at with binoculars. Summer brings with it the possibility of catching sight of the spectacular central regions of the Milky Way, with the misty swathes of countless stars that pass through Sagittarius, Scutum, and Aquila. Spring and autumn are when we can look away from our galaxy into the depths of the cosmos, and the distant galaxies that lurk in constellations such as Virgo, Coma Berenices, Triangulum, and Andromeda.

Delphinus

Sagitta

Aquila

Vulpecula

Serpens Cauda

Ophiuchus

Serpens Caput

Pisces

Pegasus

uleus

Cetus

Aries

Andromeda

Triangulum

Lacerta

Taurus

Cassiopeia

Perseus

Cepheus

Camelopardalis

Orion

Lyra

Auriga

Ursa
Major

Draco

Lynx

Gemini

Canis Minor

Leo Minor

Cancer

Canes Venatici

Boötes

Leo Minor

Coma Berenices

Leo

Virgo

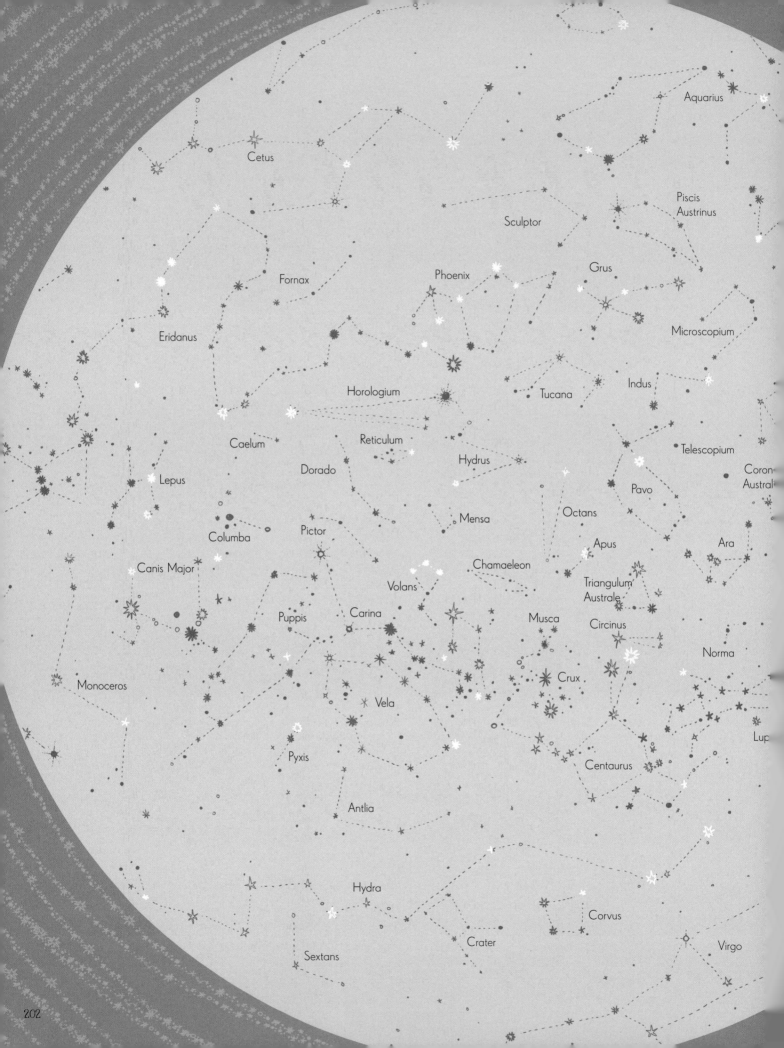

Aquarius

Cetus

Piscis
Austrinus

Sculptor

Grus

Phoenix

Microscopium

Fornax

Eridanus

Horologium

Tucana

Indus

Caelum

Reticulum

Telescopium

Dorado

Hydrus

Coron
Austral

Lepus

Mensa

Pavo

Octans

Apus

Ara

Columba

Pictor

Chamaeleon

Triangulum
Australe

Canis Major

Volans

Musca

Circinus

Puppis

Carina

Norma

Monoceros

Vela

Crux

Lup

Pyxis

Centaurus

Antlia

Hydra

Corvus

Sextans

Crater

Virgo

Southern constellations

The southern hemisphere constellation Volans represents a flying fish.

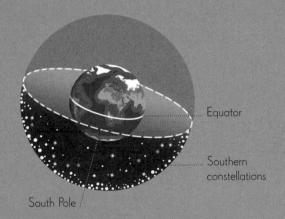

Equator

Southern constellations

South Pole

The southern hemisphere night skies contain some of the most breath-taking celestial sights it's possible to see from Earth. That's because from the southern hemisphere it's possible to see the central hub of our galaxy — in particular, the areas towards the constellations Scorpius, Sagittarius, and Ophiuchus — high in the sky. This region is absolutely bursting with bright nebulae, glittering star clusters, and dark, galactic dust clouds. The southern night skies are also where you'll find the amazing Large and Small Magellanic Clouds — in Dorado, Mensa, and Tucana — and the globular cluster Omega Centauri, in the constellation Centaurus.

Capricornus

Aquila

Sagittarius

Scutum

Serpens Cauda

Scorpius

Ophiuchus

Discovering space

Here on Earth, we have been trying to solve the mysteries of the Universe for thousands of years. These are some of our greatest achievements!

1840s
Lord Rosse observes galaxies with an enormous telescope in Birr, Ireland.

1846
The planet Neptune is discovered by Johann Galle and Heinrich d'Arrest.

1786
Astronomer Caroline Herschel finds her first comet.

1888
Williamina Fleming discovers the Horsehead Nebula.

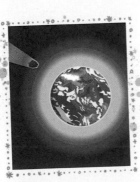

1908
A large asteroid or comet enters Earth's atmosphere and explodes over Siberia.

1912
Henrietta Leavitt makes an important discovery that helps astronomers calculate how far away distant galaxies are.

1925
Astronomer Cecilia Payne publishes ground-breaking research exploring what stars are made of.

567 BCE
Possible first recorded sighting of the Northern Lights, by Babylonian astronomers.

Around 400AD
Hypatia of Alexandria writes about astronomy and mathematics.

1054
Chinese astronomers witness a supernova, which produced the Crab Nebula we see today.

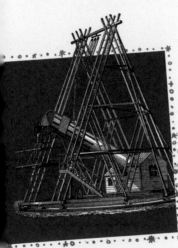

1781
William Herschel discovers the planet Uranus from Bath, England.

1610
Galileo Galilei turns a telescope toward the planet Jupiter and sees its four largest moons.

1609
Thomas Harriot makes some of the first telescopic studies of the Moon.

1543
Polish astronomer Nicolaus Copernicus publishes his theory of a Sun-centred cosmos.

1929
Astronomer Edwin Hubble discovers that the Universe is constantly expanding.

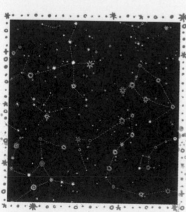

1930
Eugène Delporte draws the 88 constellations recognized today.

1930
Clyde Tombaugh discovers Pluto within the Kuiper Belt.

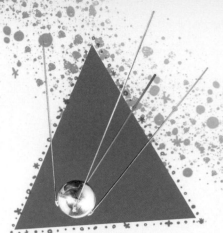

1957
The first artificial satellite, Sputnik 1, is launched by the Soviet Union.

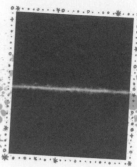

1964
Scientists discover the Cosmic Microwave Background.

1967
Astronomer Jocelyn Bell-Burnell discovers the first pulsar.

1992 to present
Astronomers study stars moving around the black hole at the Milky Way's centre.

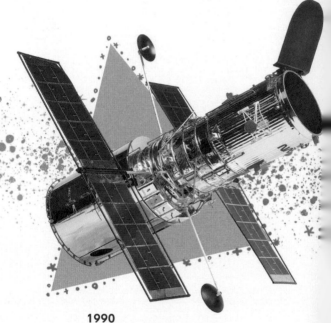

1992
The first object, besides Pluto, is discovered in the Kuiper Belt.

1990
The Hubble Space Telescope is launched by the Space Shuttle Discovery.

1999
The Chandra X-ray observatory is launched to study objects like black holes and neutron stars.

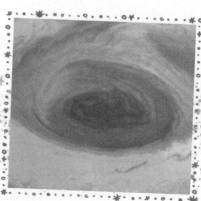

2003
The Galileo probe completes its historic exploration of Jupiter and its moons.

2003
The Spitzer Space Telescope is launched to study infrared light from the cosmos.

1969
The astronauts on the Apollo 11 mission become the first humans to step onto the Moon.

1970s–1980s
The Soviet Venera probes land on the surface of Venus.

Early 1970s
The first probes successfully land on the surface of Mars.

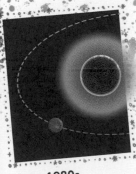

Late 1980s
Astronomers make the first discovery of planets orbiting other stars.

1987
Supernova 1987A explodes in the nearby galaxy called the Large Magellanic Cloud.

1977
The Voyager missions launch to explore the planets of the outer SolarSystem.

2004
NASA's Cassini mission enters orbit around the planet Saturn.

2004
The twin robotic rovers Spirit and Opportunity land on Mars.

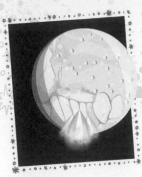

2005
The Cassini spacecraft
discovers plumes of icy
material erupting from
Saturn's moon Enceladus.

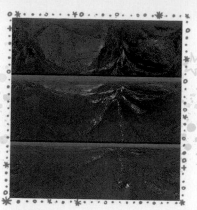

2005
The European Space
Agency's Huygens probe
parachutes to the surface
of Saturn's moon Titan.

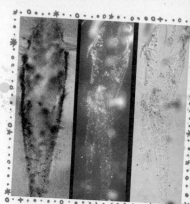

2006
The Stardust mission returns
samples of comet dust
to Earth.

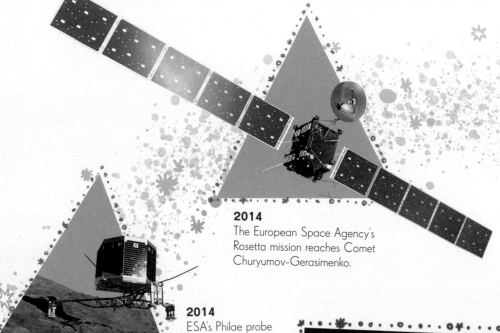

2014
The European Space Agency's
Rosetta mission reaches Comet
Churyumov-Gerasimenko.

2013
Astronomers launch the
Gaia spacecraft to map
the Milky Way.

2014
ESA's Philae probe
crash-lands on
Comet Churyumov-
Gerasimenko.

2015
The Dawn mission enters
orbit around the dwarf
planet Ceres.

2015
NASA's New Horizons
spacecraft makes the
first flyby of Pluto.

2015
Astronomers make the
first detection of gravitational
waves travelling through space.

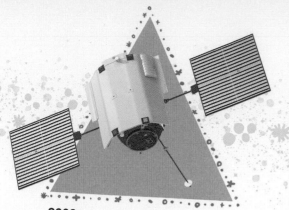

2008
The MESSENGER mission arrives at Mercury to study the smallest planet.

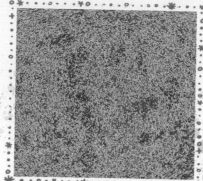

2009
The European Planck satellite creates a detailed map of the Cosmic Microwave Background.

2009
The Kepler spacecraft is launched to search for planets around other stars.

2012
Voyager 1 passes into interstellar space on its way out of the solar system.

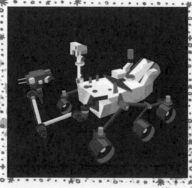

2012
NASA's rover Curiosity lands on Mars.

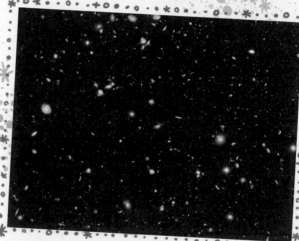

2012
The Hubble Space Telescope completes the Hubble eXtreme Deep Field image.

2017
'Oumuamua, an asteroid from another star system, is spotted passing through our solar system.

2017
The Event Horizon Telescope snaps the first picture of the silhouette of a supermassive black hole.

2019
The New Horizons spacecraft flies past the Kuiper Belt Object Arrokoth.

Glossary

asteroid a small, lumpy Solar System object usually made of either rock or metals. Many asteroids are thought to be leftover material from the formation of the planets.

Asteroid Belt, the a huge, ring-shaped region of the Solar System, located between the planets Mars and Jupiter, that is home to thousands of asteroids. The dwarf planet Ceres also orbits within the Asteroid Belt.

astronomy the study of the night sky and all the celestial objects in it, like stars, planets, and galaxies.

atmosphere the layer of gases surrounding the usually solid body of a planet or moon. The Earth's atmosphere is made mostly of nitrogen gas.

aurora glowing curtains of light that appear in the atmosphere above the polar regions of Earth. In the northern hemisphere they are called the aurora borealis, while in the southern hemisphere they are known as the aurora australis.

Big Bang, the the name given to the enigmatic event that marked the birth of the Universe. Scientists are still trying to understand what happened during the Big Bang. What we do know is that the early Universe was incredibly hot and must have quickly expanded in size, eventually becoming the vast cosmos we know today.

black hole an incredibly dense, ball-shaped region of space. Light cannot travel fast enough to escape the powerful gravitational pull of a black hole, so these mysterious objects are almost completely black.

comet a frozen Solar System object composed mostly of ice and dust. Like asteroids, comets come in a variety of lumpy shapes. Most live in the outer, colder reaches of our planetary neighbourhood. If they venture toward the Sun they can grow long tails of dust and gas.

constellation a pattern of stars in the night sky that usually represents an object, animal or mythical figure. There are 88 official constellations recognised by the International Astronomical Union today.

Cosmic Microwave Background the glow left over from the extremely hot period after the birth of the Universe.

crater a pit, shaped like a dish, in the surface of a planet, moon or other solid Solar System object. They are formed when asteroids, comets and other smaller space rocks crash into a surface, scooping out material in a fiery blast.

dwarf planet a kind of small, round, Solar System world that is not a moon or one of the eight main planets. At the moment there are five dwarf planets recognised, including Pluto and Ceres.

Earthshine light that is scattered off the clouds, oceans, and land of our planet into space, where it can faintly illuminate the night-side of the Moon's globe.

elliptical galaxy a type of galaxy that has a rounded shape similar to a sphere, or sometimes a rugby ball. Elliptical galaxies don't have spiral arms like the Milky Way.

exoplanet a planet orbiting another star outside of our own Solar System. There are likely billions of these worlds in our galaxy!

Galactic Centre the name for the very heart of our Milky Way galaxy. There is a supermassive black hole at the Galactic Centre with stars twirling around it.

galaxy a huge gathering of thousands, millions or sometimes even billions of stars that swirl together through the cosmos.

galaxy cluster a collection of multiple galaxies swarming through space in a relatively close group.

Galilean Moon the four largest moons of the planet Jupiter — Io, Europa, Ganymede, and Callisto — are known as the Galilean Moons because they were first seen by the astronomer Galileo Galilei.

Gas giants the name given to the four large planets of the outer Solar System — Jupiter, Saturn, Uranus, and Neptune — which are made largely of gas.

globular cluster a densely-packed, ball-shaped collection of many stars orbiting around a galaxy. Many of the Milky Way's globular clusters can be easily seen in the night sky with a small telescope.

gravity the force that keeps the planets orbiting the Sun, the Moon orbiting the Earth, and even vast collections of stars orbiting together as galaxies, among other things. The gravity we feel on Earth is a result of the distortion of space by the enormous mass of our planet. Larger masses — like giant planets, stars, and black holes — curve space more strongly, producing stronger gravitational pulls.

Hubble Space Telescope a large telescope, with a 2.4-metre (8-foot) wide mirror, orbiting around Earth. It has helped us to see more of the Universe, showing us pictures of glittering star clusters and distant galaxies in extraordinary detail.

hydrogen a chemical element that is found all over the cosmos. Most stars are mainly made of hydrogen, and glowing hydrogen is largely responsible for the beautiful red colour of many nebulae. Hydrogen is also found in the atmospheres of the gas giants in our Solar System.

interstellar a word used to describe things between the stars of our galaxy. For example, some of our missions to the outer Solar System are now, or will soon become interstellar travellers as they leave our planetary neighbourhood and reach interstellar space.

Kuiper Belt a large expanse of the Solar System beyond the orbit of the planet Neptune that contains many small, frozen bodies, known as Kuiper Belt Objects. Pluto orbits the Sun within the Kuiper Belt region.

lenticular galaxy a galaxy, without spiral arms, that has a shape similar to that of a simple lens.

light-year the distance travelled by a beam of light in one Earth year. Light-years are used as a way to describe the immense distances to and between far-away objects in the Universe, such as stars and galaxies.

lunar sea the smooth, dark patches on the face of the Moon made of a volcanic material called basalt.

meteor scientific name for a shooting star. A tiny fleck of space dust that shines briefly as it vaporizes while crashing into Earth's upper atmosphere.

meteoroid the name for a small grain of space dust that is floating in space.

meteorite a space rock, or a fragment of a space rock, that has made it through Earth's atmosphere to land on the surface of our planet.

Milky Way the name of our home galaxy. We see the Milky Way from the inside, as our Sun is one of the 200-400 billion stars that live in this enormous, sparkling swirl.

Moon, the the large, rocky ball that travels with Earth around the Sun. The Moon orbits our planet at a distance of roughly 384,000 km (239,000 miles).

moon the name given to the natural objects — big and small — that orbit around the various worlds, and other objects, in our Solar System and beyond.

nebula a cloud of gas and dust floating in space.

neutron star an extremely dense object, made of neutrons, that is sometimes created when a massive star explodes as a supernova.

Oort Cloud a huge sphere of icy, comet-like objects that is thought to around the Solar System.

open cluster a relatively loosely-packed bunch of stars sitting within the Milky Way.

Usually they are young stars that have formed together within a nebula. They drift through space in a group but usually spread out into the galaxy over time. There are many open clusters in the night sky that are visible using just your eyes or a good pair of binoculars.

orbit the path of one celestial object around another — such as Earth's path around the Sun, a comet's journey through the Solar System, or even the route taken by one galaxy whirling around another. The word "orbit" is also used to describe what an astronomical object is doing when it's moving on one of these paths, i.e. a moon orbits a planet.

phase the shape made by light falling on the globe of a planet or moon. The phases of our own Moon change during the month as it orbits the Earth.

planet any one of the eight main worlds in our Solar System: Mercury, Venus, Earth, Mars, Jupiter, Saturn, Uranus, and Neptune. There are planets around other stars too — see "exoplanet".

protoplanetary disc a huge, roughly flat, expanse of gas and dust orbiting a young star. Planets can form from these discs.

protostar an object forming within a nebula that may one day become a baby star if special reactions — which make it shine brightly — start within its heart.

rings grains, clumps, or large chunks of material, sometimes icy, that orbit around an astronomical object — typically a planet.

satellite the word "satellite" usually refers to the human-made objects that travel around the Earth or other bodies in the Solar System. Sometimes, though, astronomers refer to moons as the natural satellites of the planets.

Solar System the varied collection of objects — including planets, moons, asteroids, and comets — that orbit the Sun.

space the name for the vast celestial realm that lies beyond the Earth's upper atmosphere.

spiral galaxy a kind of galaxy that has a flat, circular disc composed of whirlpool like structures, known as spiral arms. The Milky Way and the nearby Andromeda Galaxy are both examples of spiral galaxies.

star an enormous ball of plasma (like a super hot gas) that shines because of reactions going on at its heart. These reactions release energy as matter is fused together in the star's core. Eventually, the reactions slow down and stop when the star dies.

supernova an extremely powerful explosion created by a dying star.

telescope a tool used to explore and study the Universe. Telescopes work by using mirrors or lenses (or sometimes both) to collect the light from objects in the night sky. They can gather more light than our eyes can, so telescopes allow astronomers to examine faint targets like faraway galaxies and nebulae. Sometimes this is done by the astronomer looking through the eyepiece of the telescope. Nowadays professional astronomers use special cameras on their telescopes to record images and other pieces of scientific information about a celestial target.

Sun, the the star at the centre of the Solar System.

Universe, the humanity's name for the space that is home to everything we know of, from the most distant galaxies known to our Moon right next door.

volcano an opening in the surface of a Solar System object where material has erupted out onto the landscape, often forming a mound or large mountain.

Visual guide

Earth's atmosphere, page 4

The night sky, page 6

Meteors, page 8

Meteorites, page 10

Auroras, page 12

Constellations, page 14

The Moon, page 16

Phases of the Moon, page 18

Lunar eclipse, page 20

Earthshine, page 22

Lunar seas, page 24

Tycho, page 26

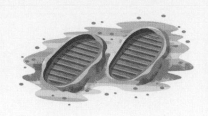

Moonwalking, page 28

The Sun, page 30

Sunspots, page 32

Rain on the Sun, page 34

Total solar eclipse, page 36

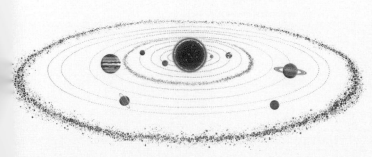

The Solar System, page 38

The rocky planets, page 40

Mercury, page 42

The transit of Mercury, page 44

Caloris Basin, page 46

Venus, page 48

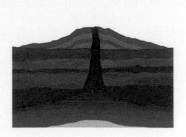

Volcanoes on Venus, page 50

Deadly clouds, page 52

Mars, page 54

Valles Marineris, page 56

Olympus Mons, page 58

Martian dust devils, page 60

Water on Mars, page 62

Exploring Mars, page 64

The moons of Mars, page 66

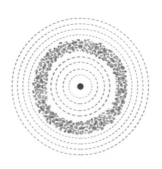

Asteroids, page 68

Ceres, page 70

The gas giants, page 72

Jupiter, page 74

Swirling clouds, page 76

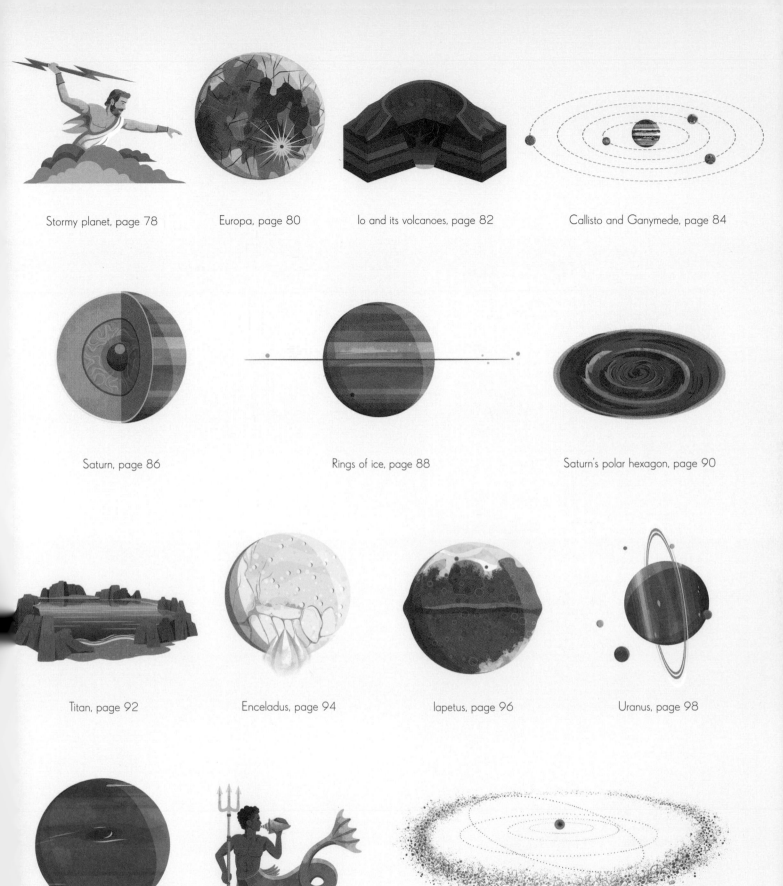

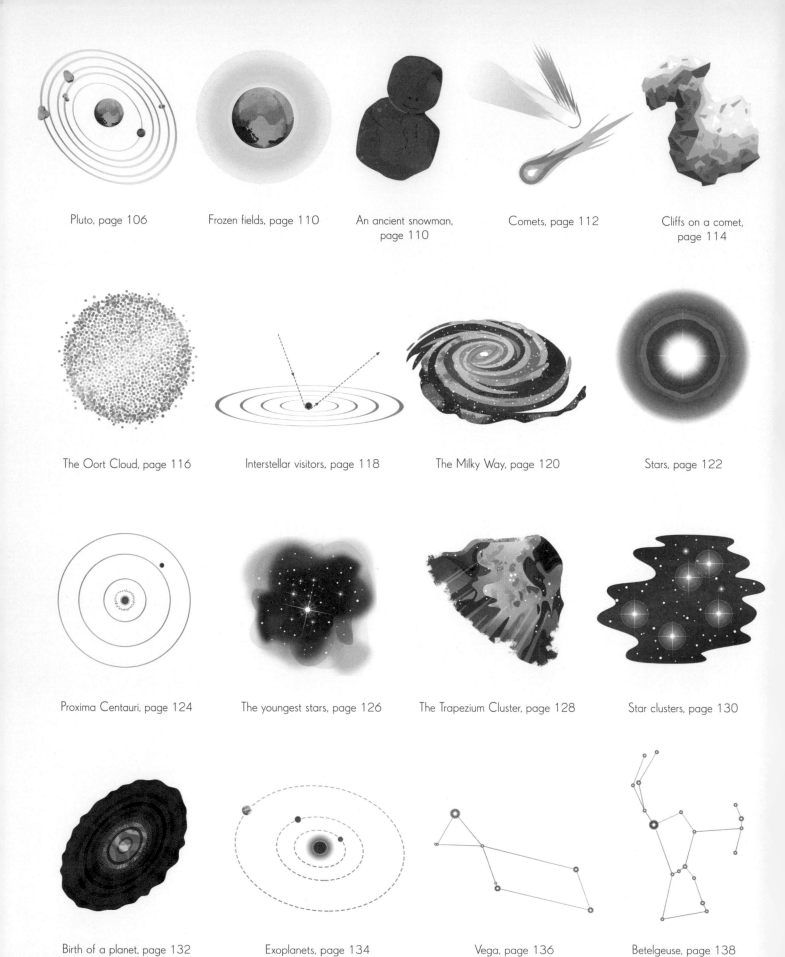

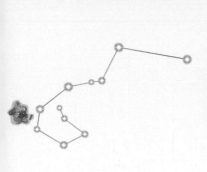

Eta Carinae, page 140

Supernova, page 142

Neutron star, page 144

Black hole, page 146

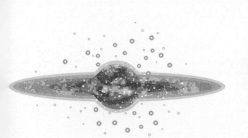

Globular cluster, page 148

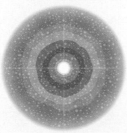

Nebula, page 150

Emission nebula, page 152

Planetary nebula, page 154

Dark nebula, page 156

Reflection nebula, page 158

Galactic Centre, page 160

The Pillars of Creation, page 162

Supernova remnant, page 164

Galaxies, page 166

The Local Group, page 168

Dwarf galaxy, page 170

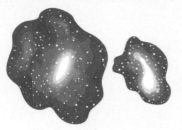

The Magellanic Clouds, page 172

The Andromeda Galaxy, page 174

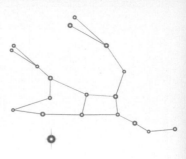

Starburst galaxy, page 176

Spiral galaxy, page 178

Lenticular galaxy, page 180

Elliptical galaxy, page 182

Interacting galaxies, page 184

Stephan's Quintet, page 186

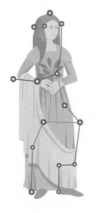

The Local Supercluster, page 188

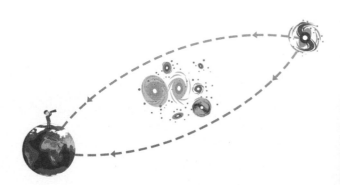

Gravitational lens, page 190

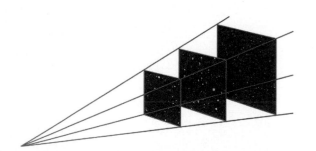

Gazing into the past, page 192

The cosmic web, page 194

The cosmic glow, page 196

Beyond this book

I hope that after reading this book you can see what a wondrous Universe we live in. It's full of great beauty, breath-taking scale, and captivating puzzles. Some of the questions scientists have about the workings of stars, planets, and even whole galaxies may well be solved in your lifetime. But there will always be more to come.

You'll no doubt have questions of your own as you continue to explore the Universe. Don't be afraid to ask them! This is how we learn and find out about the world around us, and beyond. Perhaps one day you'll help to solve some of these exciting cosmic mysteries...

Will Gater

Index

Project editor Abby Aitcheson
Designer Charlotte Jennings
Jacket co-ordinator Issy Walsh
Senior jacket designer Elle Ward
Production editor Dragana Puvacic
Production controller Barbara Ossowska
Project picture researcher Sakshi Saluja
DTP designer Vijay Kandwal
Managing editor Jonathan Melmoth
Managing art editor Diane Peyton Jones
Publishing director Sarah Larter

First published in Great Britain in 2020 by
Dorling Kindersley Limited
DK, One Embassy Gardens, 8 Viaduct Gardens,
London SW11 7BW

Copyright © 2020 Dorling Kindersley Limited
A Penguin Random House Company
10 9 8 7 6 5 4 3 2 1
001-316659-Sept/2020

A CIP catalogue record for this book
is available from the British Library.
ISBN: 978-0-2414-1247-3

Printed and bound in China

For the curious
www.dk.com

DK would like to thank: Caroline Hunt for
proofreading, Daniel Long for the feature
illustrations, and Angela Rizza for the pattern
and cover illustrations.

About the author: Will Gater is an
astronomer, journalist, and science presenter.
He has written several popular astronomy
books and is an experienced observational
astronomer and astrophotographer.

Important notice: Observing the Sun directly or through any kind of optical device can cause blindness. The author and publishers cannot accept any responsibility for readers who ignore this advice.

Picture Credits
The publisher would like to thank the following for their kind permission to reproduce their photographs:
(Key: a-above; b-below/bottom; c-centre; f-far; l-left; r-right; t-top)
4-5 Jan Erik Paulsen. 6-7 ESO: Y. Beletsky. **9 Science Photo Library:** Walter Pacholka, Astropics. **10 ESO:** H. Pedersen / M.Zamani. **12-13 NASA:** (b). **14 Science Photo Library:** Eckhard Slawik. **17 NASA:** NOAA. **18-19 Science Photo Library:** Eckhard Slawik. **20 Will Gater. 23 NASA:** Ken Fisher, Johnson Space Center. **25 NASA. 26 ESA / Hubble:** NASA, ESA, D. Ehrenreich (Institut de Planétologie et d'Astrophysique de Grenoble (IPAG) / CNRS / Université Joseph Fourier). **28-29 ESO:** NASA (b). **30 ESA. 31 NASA:** SDO / AIA / S. Wiessinger. **32 Stockholm University:** Mats Löfdahl, ISP / Göran Scharmer, ISP. **34-35 NASA:** GSFC / SDO. **36 NASA. 37 ESO:** P. Horálek / Solar Wind Sherpas project. **40 NASA:** Johns Hopkins University Applied Physics Laboratory / Carnegie Institution of Washington (cl); JPL (tc). **40-41 NASA:** Goddard Space Flight Center Image by Reto Stöckli (c). **41 NASA:** JPL / USGS (cra). **42 NASA:** Johns Hopkins University Applied Physics Laboratory / Carnegie Institution of Washington. **43 NASA:** Goddard Space Flight Center (c). **44-45 NASA:** Goddard Space Flight Center. **47 NASA:** Johns Hopkins University Applied Physics Laboratory / Carnegie Institution of Washington. **49 NASA:** Goddard Space Flight Center Scientific Visualization Studio. **50-51 NASA:** JPL. **52 NASA. 54-55 ESA. 56-57 NASA:** JPL-Caltech. **58 NASA:** JPL / Malin Space Science Systems. **60-61 NASA:** HiRISE, MRO, LPL (U. Arizona). **63 ESA:** DLR / FU Berlin, CC BY-SA 3.0 IGO. **64-65 NASA:** JPL-Caltech / MSSS. **66 NASA:** JPL-Caltech / University of Arizona (tl). **67 NASA:** JPL-Caltech / University of Arizona (b). **68 NASA:** JPL-Caltech / UCLA / MPS / DLR / IDA (tl); JPL (tr). **69 NASA. 70-71 NASA:** Goddard Space Flight Center. **72 NASA:** ESA, and A. Simon (NASA Goddard) (tl). **73 NASA:** The Hubble Heritage Team (STScI / AURA)Acknowledgment: R.G. French (Wellesley College), J. Cuzzi (NASA / Ames), L. Dones (SwRI), and J. Lissauer (NASA / Ames) (t); JPL-Caltech (cr); JPL (bc). **74 NASA:** JPL (ca). **75 NASA:** Enhanced image by Gerald Eichstädt and Justin Cowart based on images provided courtesy of NASA / JPL-Caltech / SwRI / MSSS. **76 NASA:** JPL-Caltech / SwRI / MSSS / Gerald Eichstadt / Sean Doran © CC NC SA. **79 NASA:** JPL-Caltech / SwRI / MSSS / Gerald Eichstadt / Sean Doran © CC NC SA. **80 NASA:** JPL-Caltech / SETI Institute. **83 NASA:** JPL / University of Arizona. **85 NASA:** JPL / DLR (tl); JPL / DLR (cr). **86-87 NASA:** JPL-Caltech / Space Science Institute. **86 NASA:** JPL-Caltech (bc). **88 NASA:** JPL. **90 NASA:** JPL-Caltech / SSI / Hampton University. **92-93 NASA:** ESA / JPL / University of Arizona. **95 NASA:** JPL / Space Science Institute. **96-97 NASA:** JPL / Space Science Institute. **98 ESA / Hubble:** Hubble & NASA, L. Lamy / Observatoire de Paris. **101 NASA:** JPL. **102-103 NASA:** JPL / USGS. **107 NASA:** Johns Hopkins University Applied Physics Laboratory / Southwest Research Institute. **108-109 NASA:** JHUAPL / SwRI. **111 NASA:** Johns Hopkins University Applied Physics Laboratory / Southwest Research Institute / Roman Tkachenko. **113 ESO:** E. Slawik. **115 ESA:** Rosetta / MPS for OSIRIS Team MPS / UPD / LAM / IAA / SSO / INTA / UPM / DASP / IDA. **118-119 NASA and The Hubble Heritage Team (AURA/STScI):** NASA, ESA, and J. Olmsted and F. Summers (STScI). **120-121 NASA:** JPL-Caltech / ESA / CXC / STScI. **122 NASA and The Hubble Heritage Team (AURA/STScI):** NASA, ESA, and H. Richer and J. Heyl (University of British Columbia, Vancouver, Canada);. 124 NASA: Penn State University (bc). **125 ESA / Hubble:** NASA. **126 NASA and The Hubble Heritage Team (AURA/STScI):** NASA, ESA, the Hubble Heritage Team (STScI / AURA), and IPHAS. **128 ESO:** IDA / Danish 1.5 m / R. Gendler, J.-E. Ovaldsen, and A. Hornstrup. **130-131 NASA and The Hubble Heritage Team (AURA/STScI):** NASA, ESA and AURA / Caltech. **132-133 ESO:** L. Calçada. **134 NASA:** Goddard Space Flight Center / Chris Smith. **135 NASA:** Goddard Space Flight Center / Chris Smith (tr); Goddard Space Flight Center / Chris Smith (cla). **136 Stephen Rahn. 138 ESO:** ALMA (NAOJ / NRAO) / E. O'Gorman / P. Kervella. **140 NASA:** ESA, N. Smith (University of Arizona) and J. Morse (BoldlyGo Institute). **143 ESO:** NASA / ESA Hubble Space Telescope, Chandra X-Ray observatory. **144 NASA and The Hubble Heritage Team (AURA/STScI):** NASA and ESA; J. Hester (ASU) and M. Weisskopf (NASA / MSFC). **146-147 Science Photo Library:** EHT Collaboration / European Southern Observatory. **148-149 ESO. 151 ESO:** Zdenek Bardon (tl); Y. Beletsky (tr). NASA and The Hubble Heritage Team (AURA/STScI): NASA, ESA, and the Hubble Heritage Team (STScI / AURA) (cl); NASA, ESA, and STScI (br); NASA, ESA, J. DePasquale (STScI), and R. Hurt (Caltech / IPAC) (bl). **152 Robert Gendler. 154 ESO. NASA:** JPL-Caltech / ESA, the Hubble Heritage Team (STScI / AURA) (cl). **155 NASA and The Hubble Heritage Team (AURA/STScI):** Bruce Balick (University of Washington), Jason Alexander (University of Washington), Arsen Hajian (U.S. Naval Observatory), Yervant Terzian (Cornell University), Mario Perinotto (University of Florence, Italy), Patrizio Patriarchi (Arcetri Observatory, Italy) and NASA (tl). NASA: CXC / SAO; Optical: NASA / STScI (cra). **156-157 NOAO / AURA / NSF:** T.A.Rector (NOAO / AURA / NSF) and Hubble Heritage Team (STScI / AURA / NASA). **159 ESO:** Igor Chekalin. **160-161 NASA:** JPL-Caltech / S. Stolovy (Spitzer Science Center / Caltech). **163 NASA and The Hubble Heritage Team (AURA/STScI):** NASA, ESA, and the Hubble Heritage Team (STScI / AURA). **164-165 Ken Crawford. 166 ESO:** Chris Mihos (Case Western Reserve University) (br). NASA and The Hubble Heritage Team (AURA/STScI): NASA, ESA, S. Bianchi (Università degli Studi Roma Tre University), A. Laor (Technion-Israel Institute of Technology), and M. Chiaberge (ESA, STScI, and JHU) (t); NASA, ESA, A. Aloisi (STScI / ESA), and The Hubble Heritage (STScI / AURA)-ESA / Hubble Collaboration (bl). **168 ESO.** NASA and The Hubble Heritage Team (AURA/STScI): NASA, ESA, and Z. Levy (STScI) (crb). **169 ESO. Robert Gendler. 171 ESO:** Digitized Sky Survey 2. 172-173 NASA: JPL-Caltech / M. Meixner (STScI) & the SAGE Legacy Team. **174-175 Robert Gendler. 177 Johannes Schedler** (panther-observatory.com). **178 NASA and The Hubble Heritage Team (AURA/STScI):** NASA, ESA, and the Hubble Heritage (STScI / AURA)-ESA / Hubble Collaboration;. **180-181 NASA and The Hubble Heritage Team (AURA/STScI):** NASA, ESA, and The Hubble Heritage Team (STScI / AURA);. **182 NASA and The Hubble Heritage Team (AURA/STScI):** NASA, ESA, and The Hubble Heritage Team (STScI / AURA);. **184-185 ESA / Hubble:** NASA, Holland Ford (JHU), the ACS Science Team. **186-187 ESA:** NASA and the Hubble SM4 ERO Team. **189 Kees Scherer. 190 NASA and The Hubble Heritage Team (AURA/STScI):** NASA, ESA, and J. Lotz and the HFF Team (STScI). **192-193 NASA:** ESA; G. Illingworth, D. Magee, and P. Oesch, University of California, Santa Cruz; R. Bouwens, Leiden University; and the HUDF09 Team). **193 ESA / Hubble:** NASA, G. Illingworth, D. Magee, and P. Oesch (University of California, Santa Cruz), R. Bouwens (Leiden University), Z. Levay (STScI) and the HUDF09 Team (b). **194-195 IllustrisTNG collaboration:** D. Nelson. **196-197 ESA:** Planck Collaboration. **204 Alamy Stock Photo:** Chronicle (cl); The History Collection (c); Historic Images (c/Heinrich Louis d Arrest); GL Archive (cr); Granger Historical Picture Archive (cb); Science History Images (crb). NOAO / AURA / NSF: T.A.Rector (NOAO / AURA / NSF) and Hubble Heritage Team (STScI / AURA / NASA) (clb). **205 Alamy Stock Photo:** Archivio GBB (tc); gameover (cl); IanDagnall Computing (c); The Picture Art Collection (c/Thomas Harriot); Science History Images (cr); GL Archive (cb). NASA and The Hubble Heritage Team (AURA/STScI): NASA, ESA, J. DePasquale (STScI), and R. Hurt (Caltech / IPAC) (tr). Science Photo Library: Emilio Segre Visual Archives / American Institute of Physics (clb). **206 Dorling Kindersley:** Andy Crawford (cr). ESO. NASA: CXC / NGST (clb); JPL / Cornell University (cb); JPL-Caltech / R. Hurt (SSC) (crb). Science Photo Library: NASA (tc/Cosmic); Sputnik (tc); Robin Scagell (tr). **207 ESO:** NASA (tl). NASA. Science Photo Library: Russian Academy of Sciences / Detlev Van Ravenswaay (cra); Sputnik (tc). **208 Alamy Stock Photo:** National Geographic Image Collection (tr). Science History Images (cr). ESA: C. Carreau / ATG medialab (c). NASA: ESA / JPL / University of Arizona (tc); JPL-Caltech / UCLA / MPS / DLR / IDA (clb/Ceres); Johns Hopkins University Applied Physics Laboratory / Southwest Research Institute (cb). Science Photo Library: European Space Agency / ATG Medialab (clb). **209 Alamy Stock Photo:** Science History Images (cl). Dreamstime.com: Konstantin Shaklein (tl). ESA: Planck Collaboration (tl). NASA and The Hubble Heritage Team (AURA/STScI): NASA, ESA, and J. Olmsted and F. Summers (STScI) (clb). NASA: Ames / J. Jenkins (cra); ESA; G. Illingworth, D. Magee, and P. Oesch, University of California, Santa Cruz; R. Bouwens, Leiden University; and the HUDF09 Team) (cr). Science Photo Library: EHT Collaboration / European Southern Observatory (cb)
Cover images: Front: **Fotolia:** Eevl tl; **NASA and The Hubble Heritage Team (AURA/STScI):** NASA, ESA and AURA / Caltech crb, NASA, ESA, J. DePasquale (STScI), and R. Hurt (Caltech / IPAC) ca; **NASA:** ESA, N. Smith (University of Arizona) and J. Morse (BoldlyGo Institute) br, Johns Hopkins University Applied Physics Laboratory / Carnegie Institution of Washington tr, JPL-Caltech / ESA, the Hubble Heritage Team (STScI / AURA) cra, STScI / AURA cla; **Science Photo Library:** Walter Pacholka, Astropics cr
All other images © Dorling Kindersley Limited. For further information see: www.dkimages.com